R

SERIES EDITORS: Leslie J Francis and Jeff Astley

SHAPING THE TOOLS

Study Skills in Theology

Ruth Ackroyd

and

David Major

DARTON · LONGMAN + TODD

First published in 1999 by
Darton, Longman and Todd Ltd
1 Spencer Court
140-142 Wandsworth High Street
London SW18 4JJ

ISBN 0-232-52342-8

A catalogue record for this book is available from the British Library.

Designed by Sandie Boccacci
Phototypeset in Minion by Intype London Ltd
Printed and bound in Great Britain by
Page Bros, Norwich, Norfolk

CONTENTS

PREFACE

At the beginning of the third millennium a new mood is sweeping through the Christian churches. This mood is reflected in a more radical commitment to discipleship among a laity who wish to be theologically informed and fully equipped for Christian ministry in the secular world.

Exploring Faith: theology for life is designed for people who want to take Christian theology seriously. Taken seriously, Christian theology engages the mind, involves the heart, and seeks active expression in the way we live. Those who explore their faith in this way are beginning to shape a theology for life.

Exploring Faith: theology for life is rooted in the individual experience of the world and in the ways through which God is made known in the world. Such experience is related to and interpreted in the light of the Christian tradition. Each volume in the series takes a key aspect of theology, and explores this aspect in dialogue with the readers' own experience. Each volume is written by a scholar who has clear authority in the area of theology discussed and who takes seriously the ways in which busy adults learn.

The volumes are suitable for all those who wish to learn more about the Christian faith and ministry, including those who have already taken Christian basic courses (such as *Alpha* and *Emmaus*) and have been inspired to undertake further study, those preparing to take theology as an undergraduate course, and those already engaged on degree programmes. The volumes have been developed for individuals to work on alone or for groups to study together.

Already groups of Christians are using the *Exploring Faith: theology for life* series throughout the United Kingdom, linked by an exciting initiative pioneered jointly by the Anglican dioceses, the Board of Education of the Church and World Division and the Ministry Division of the Archbishops' Council of the Church of England, the National

Society and the Church Colleges. Used in this way each volume can earn credits towards one of the Church Colleges' Certificates and provide access to degree level study. Further information about the Church Colleges' Certificate Programme is provided on page 124.

The Church Colleges' Certificate Programme integrates well with the lifelong learning agenda which now plays such a crucial role in educational priorities. Learning Christians can find their way into degree-bearing programmes through this series *Exploring Faith: theology for life* linked with the Church Colleges' Certificates.

In preparing a series of this kind, much work is done behind the scenes. Financial and staff support have been generously given by the Ministry Division. Thanks are due to Marilyn Parry for the vision of bringing together the Aston materials and the Anglican Church Colleges of Higher Education. Thanks also should go to the Aston staff and the original authors for being willing to make the materials available for reworking. We are also grateful for financial support from the following Church Colleges: Chester College; Christ Church University College, Canterbury; The College of St Mark and St John, Plymouth; St Martin's College, Lancaster; Trinity College Carmarthen; and Whitelands College (Roehampton Institute). Without the industry, patience, perception, commitment and skill of Ruth Ackroyd this series would have remained but a dream.

The series editors wish to express their personal thanks to colleagues who have helped them shape the series identity, especially Diane Drayson, Ros Fane, Evelyn Jackson, Anne Rees and Morag Reeve, and to the individual authors who have produced high-quality text on schedule and so generously accepted firm editorial direction. The editorial work has been supported by the North of England Institute for Christian Education and the Centre for Theology and Education at Trinity College Carmarthen.

Leslie J Francis
Jeff Astley

INTRODUCTION

The aim of this book is to equip the reader with some of the tools that are necessary to undertake studies in theology and ministry. Before undertaking any worthwhile task, it is as well to be prepared. This book seeks to assist with that preparation. We hope that you will enjoy the learning that it points you towards as much as you will enjoy studying theology itself. We hope that it will open up new horizons for you and new ways of understanding, engaging you at a personal level as much as your later study will. You may find that it feeds and challenges faith, and enables you to discover new gifts and abilities and to grow in confidence.

The book has been written principally to cater for adult learners who are new to higher education. It recognises that, for many of its readers, some considerable time may have elapsed since they last undertook serious study. Equally, the authors consider that readers entering higher education direct from school will find the book of real benefit.

The book is divided into two sections. In the first section (chapters 1 to 5), Ruth Ackroyd deals with the practical concerns of study skills for adult learners who may be new to higher education. She anticipates the questions they will ask as they encounter what may be, for them, a new and, at first, rather strange and bewildering environment. In dealing with those questions, she has worked with a number of adult learners and colleagues in order to test out ideas and to gauge the usefulness of the guidance she offers. In particular she would like to thank Rita, Cynthia, Terry and Robert Evans, the students and staff who have allowed her to use their work, and Yvonne Lawrence, Fran Kenny, Vicki Bulgin and Nancy Ackroyd who have commented on drafts of chapters.

In the second section (chapters 6 to 10), David Major introduces adult learners to a range of skills, ideas and theories which can be drawn on to support them in their development as higher education students. These skills and ideas are related to the practical, everyday concerns of study and to life beyond the academy.

The authors consider these two sections of the book to be complementary. Both sections seek to combine the twin aims of student-centredness (working from and with the concerns of the learners) and academic integrity (working from and with education theory and practice). They do not necessarily envisage the book being read sequentially. Their hope is that learners will familiarise themselves with its contents and then use it as a resource as and when it is needed. Thus, faced with writing an essay, there may be the need to consult chapter 3 before commencing the preparatory reading and then chapter 4 and chapter 6 before writing the essay. Some chapters may only need to be read once, for example, chapter 2, while others may need to be referred to more frequently as and when the occasion arises, for example, chapter 5 and chapter 7. In some instances, individuals may already have an understanding of the area that is being covered. Clearly, in such cases they can pass over the material summarily and move to something new. The book caters for a wide readership and, therefore, readers should not be surprised if they find some material with which they are already familiar.

The authors have taught in higher education for over fifteen years with earlier experience in secondary and further education. They are committed to widening access and increasing participation in higher education. They teach students who have entered higher education straight from school and also mature (returning) students whose ages range from 21 to 70 (at least!), some of whom are returning to formal education after a break of over 30 years. They teach full-time students who frequently have part-time jobs, and part-time students, many of whom have full-time jobs. Some of their students are studying in order to equip themselves for a variety of Christian ministries, both lay and ordained; others are studying simply because they are fascinated by the subject of theology. Some have faith positions other than Christian while others are Christian; some are agnostic and some are atheist. Whatever their faith or life stance, the authors value the fact that their students hold in common a belief in the value and potential of every human being, the importance of search for meaning in life, and a sense of shared responsibility for the world in which we all live. This book is for all of these students.

1. TAKING STOCK: AN AUDIT OF LEARNING

Introduction

The image of stock-taking comes from the commercial world and describes the task of assessing current resources, deciding what items need to be replenished and what new articles are needed. It is a task that is familiar to most people, for example, preparing to do the weekly shopping or organising the youth club tuck shop. Taking stock is also an important exercise when beginning a course of study.

In this chapter we 'take stock' in five areas, working from general to more detailed tasks. We:

- encourage you to identify and value the learning that you bring to any new task;
- seek to identify goals, in order to help you to set priorities and organise your studies;
- identify some practical tasks in preparation for study;
- explain time and task management and relate them to each other, using a number of practical examples;
- examine in more detail what it means to analyse tasks and to set targets.

Reflecting on experience

If you are beginning a new course of study, what previous learning are you bringing to the course?

As you hear about the skills of learning (for example, listening, reading, making notes, writing essays) do you think, 'I'm no good at ...'? If so, how would you be tempted to complete that sentence? You might like to write in its place 'I can become better at ...'

Do you have examples of how new learning, now or in the past, has challenged or changed your previously held views?

Identifying and valuing previous learning

The title of the chapter refers to the skills and previous learning that you bring with you to the task of learning. Some of you will approach a new learning venture with excitement, anticipation and confidence. For others of you these emotions may be mixed with some trepidation; you may feel that you know little or have few skills. However, more often than not we all know more, and have more skills, than we give ourselves credit for. One of the recurring themes of this book will be to encourage you to identify the skills and learning that you already possess and to use these as a springboard for further learning. (This idea will be explored further in chapter 7.)

Usually during a course, new learning builds on previous learning in an obvious and enjoyable way. At other times you may have to unlearn lessons from the past that otherwise may form barriers to future learning. These may be as simple as incorrect facts that can be easily corrected; more complex barriers, however, such as negative attitudes towards oneself as a learner, may be more difficult to change. For example, some students may come with bad learning experiences from the past leading them to say things like, 'I'm no good at ...' It may need a lot of determination and encouragement to substitute and believe the phrases, 'I am good at ...' or 'I can become better at ...'

Often new learning about theology, the Bible and the church opens up, for the student, new and different ways of understanding ideas and beliefs, some of which may, in the past, have been problematic. When this happens, learning is like opening a window onto a new world: exciting and exhilarating. It is also sometimes the case that new learning challenges previous learning and deeply held convictions. When this happens, learning can be painful and lead to uncertainty about previously held beliefs. It is, therefore, important to develop two capacities in order to handle new learning. These are: *an open mind*, to give serious attention to new information and arguments presented to you in teaching and reading; and *critical judgement*, to be able to weigh up the evidence for and against the different views expressed and to decide what you think is the best conclusion and why. At the same time, you will gain a better understanding of the reasons why others may disagree with you.

Identifying goals

Having recognised the significance of past learning, we now look ahead to identify some goals for learning. The purpose of this section is to establish what your goals are and why you have them. You may be reading this book because it has been recommended to you by a tutor as you begin a course of study run by your church, diocese or college, or because you want help with a particular aspect of your studies. These are two different goals. The latter need is very specific and you may already have identified the chapter that you want to read and be ready to turn straight to it. The former group, those beginning their studies, may have a number of related goals. These might include one or more of the following, and especially the last one:

• to complete the course successfully in order to proceed to the next stage;
• to learn as much as possible in order to use the knowledge and skills gained;
• *to enjoy the course.*

Different goals will affect the approach to learning that is taken. Those who wish to complete the course successfully in order to get to the next stage will focus on doing what is necessary to be successful in order to progress. We might call this a *strategic approach.*

Those who want to learn as much as possible in order to use their knowledge and skills will focus on a comprehensive and detailed approach. We might call this a *deep learning approach.*

Although it is hoped that all students will enjoy their studies, those students who are studying as a leisure pursuit will focus on the parts of the learning that they enjoy most. We might call this a *selective approach.*

You may identify with one or more, or indeed all, of these aims, or have different ones. The important point is to identify them, identify the reasons for them, and be aware of the effect that they will have on your learning.

EXERCISE
Setting goals and articulating them can be an important aid to learning. Write down your own goals for the course you are embarking on.

Practical tasks

There are some, perhaps obvious, practical tasks to decide on before you begin your studies. These include finding a place to study and ensuring that you have the necessary equipment.

It is, of course, very comfortable to read a book while sitting in an armchair, but the atmosphere may not be conducive to serious study. If the radio is playing in the background, or the television is on, it makes the task of concentration that much harder. Usually when reading for academic study you need to be involved in active learning that requires you to make notes. Certainly when it comes to writing an essay you will need some sort of dedicated space. A room of your own or a designated study space is ideal. It may seem obvious, but it is worth saying that you will need quiet and heat and light as well as a desk or table and chair and bookshelves. Association of place with certain activities can provide a powerful psychological motivation towards that activity. Therefore, if you begin to associate your room or designated space with periods of study, it will help you to focus your mind on your work as you use it.

It is also important to have the right equipment available: paper and pens, pencils, rubber and highlighter, but also files, plastic wallets and possibly labels. It is also important, when time is precious, to be able to find work straightaway, without having to search through a heap of papers.

Two other resources are important. Access to books is vital and more will be said about this in the next chapter. Another resource to consider is a computer or word processor. This is helpful not only for organising notes and writing essays but also, if possible, for access to the Internet and e-mail. Computers are expensive items but are becoming increasingly important in education.

Time management and task management

You are used to managing time and tasks. You organise both of these daily without really thinking about it. Nevertheless, embarking on studies often introduces new tasks, for example, academic reading and writing essays, that require considerable practice and familiarity before you are able to organise them confidently into a routine. Lack of experience of these tasks can create time management problems, for example when the first essay for a course is due to be submitted.

Time management

Take Claire as an example. She is studying on a course which requires two hours of attendance per week for ten weeks and two pieces of assessed work, each equivalent to 1,500 to 2,000 words. Unfortunately, Claire had not noted in her diary when the essay was due, and the submission date therefore came upon her rather suddenly. She had some difficulty in deciding which essay title to choose, and had not done any initial reading or thinking in order to help her to make a choice. When, therefore, Claire was invited to present her ideas for the essay to her tutor and fellow students at a workshop on preparing essays, it was difficult for them to offer suggestions and advice because the ideas were vague and woolly. The night before the essay was due to be submitted, Claire was still not sure whether she had understood the title properly and she did not have the books that she needed. Still, she had to write something. She had found that it really did take much longer to write an essay than she had anticipated. She wished that she had started earlier.

EXERCISE

Perhaps you have never experienced the same problem as Claire but, for most, the last-minute essay is a common problem. Consider what Claire's difficulties are and how she might address them. Make a note of your answers and compare them with the notes below.

Claire's main problem was with time management. She had not noted in her diary the submission date for her essay and had not worked back from that date to plan the time needed for preparing and writing the essay. The other problems stemmed from this. Faced with a choice of essay title, she should have considered all the titles and then chosen the one that most interested her. She then needed to search for books in the library to ensure that she had the necessary resources. Time was then needed for reading to check that the subject interested her, and to prepare for the group discussion. If she had done all this, she would have received advice and encouragement; she would also by this time have acquired some books to resource the essay. The answer to the problem of knowing how much time is needed to write an essay comes with practice, but a basic rule is to begin the planning early.

It may be helpful to think more generally about time management in relation to Claire's difficulties and her situation. Time management begins with identifying what time is available for different activities. For example, Claire is in paid employment three days a week; she has two school-age children and is not able to study in the evening before about 9.00p.m. Weekends are taken up with the family.

Claire decides on the following pattern of study:

Monday	9.00a.m. to 5.00p.m. paid employment
	9.00p.m. to 10.30p.m. study
Tuesday	9.00a.m. to 5.00p.m. paid employment
	7.00p.m. to 9.00p.m. theology course
Wednesday	9.00a.m. to 5.00p.m. paid employment
	9.00p.m. to 10.30p.m. study
Thursday	10.00a.m. to 1.00p.m. study
	2.00p.m. to 3.30p.m. housework
	9.00p.m. to 10.30p.m. study
Friday	10.00a.m. to 1.00p.m. study
	afternoon – weekly shop
Weekend	free

Claire has chosen to study on three evenings from 9.00 to 10.30p.m. and on the two mornings when she is not doing paid work. She may have found that she works best in the mornings and she may even decide to try working from 6.30 to 7.30a.m. instead of in the evening. She has decided that it is important to keep the weekends free for the family. Other students, of course, have other priorities and commitments, but this example raises the issues of time management in relation to commitments to work, family, friends and yourself. Of course, it may be impossible to design a regular weekly timetable if every week is different. Time management in those circumstances means recognising the time when you do have a choice about what you might do and then managing that time in relation to commitments. If there is a weakness or limitation with time management, it is that giving time to a task does not ensure its completion. It is therefore necessary to combine time management with task management.

Task management

As a second example we will take John's problem of task management in relation to essay writing. John is not sure which of two essays to attempt, so he has found three books on each subject and when he has finished reading all of them, he will make his decision. He has spent many hours reading and it has taken longer than expected to finish all the books. He is still faced with the decision about which essay to choose and spends more time coming to a decision. Having chosen his essay title, he has taken more books out of the library; he finds the reading interesting but wonders where it is all leading. However, he comforts himself with the thought that he is certainly working long hours at his studies. Unfortunately, the weekend before the essay is due in, he finds that he has many pages of notes and no clear idea of how to proceed. The essay topic seems a bit boring now, he has read so much, perhaps he will go and make a fourth cup of coffee before trying to sort out his notes again ...

EXERCISE

You may feel that the description above is a caricature or you may identify at least with parts of it. Consider John's problems and how he might address them. Compare your answers with the notes below.

John has set plenty of time aside to study, but he has fallen victim to the maxim that says that any task expands to fill the time available. He might find it helpful to break down the one task of writing an essay into its several parts: choosing a title, researching, planning, writing, and editing.

A next stage might be to decide on the time necessary to complete each stage and allot a minimum and maximum time to it. It might look like this:

- choosing a title $\frac{1}{2}$–1hr;
- researching   8–16hrs;
- planning $\frac{1}{2}$–1hr;
- writing   3–6hrs;
- editing $\frac{1}{2}$–1hr.

The time parameters give considerable flexibility but also act as a constraint in preventing the task from getting out of hand.

EXERCISE

Set yourself an exercise in time and task management. Begin by reviewing the previous week, if it was fairly typical. Work through each day noting what you did and how long you gave to each task. It may be helpful to work in units no smaller than 1 hour. You should be able to account for all 24 hours of each day.

The next stage is to plan the week ahead. Using a blank sheet of paper, fill in the days of the week and divide up each day into morning, afternoon and evening. Begin by noting the tasks that have to be done; not just study but also work, family and leisure commitments. If they are restricted to a certain time or day of the week, then fill them in and add the time that each takes.

Next, you need to fill in your study tasks and the time that you will spend on them.

To give you a sense of what is expected of full-time students here are some of the guidelines for courses in higher education. Those studying on undergraduate degree programmes are expected to do about 1,200 hours of study per year. Each programme is divided into a set number of courses per year and the numbers vary between institutions. Full-time students might expect to do about 30–35 hours of study each week. Part-time students, therefore, might do as little as seven hours or as many as 20 hours of study per week, depending on the intensity of their programme. You need to be clear about what specific study is required of you. This can usually be established by asking your tutor and by finding out about the nature of the formal assessment (essay/exam/report or presentations) and the week-by-week study tasks, for example, reading core texts, library research, that need to be completed.

In order to plan these hours of study it may be helpful to bear in mind the times of day when you work best. If you do not know when these are, then experiment for a fortnight or so. It may be helpful to keep a diary and to fill in the tasks and the time, and to break these down into smaller units, so that study time is clearly focused on a task to be completed. It is important to set realistic tasks for the time available. In order to do this you need to begin to find out how long it takes to complete certain tasks. For example, how long does it take you to read ten pages of a text book? Sometimes, perhaps quite often, the study plan will need to be revised because of emergencies or because a task takes longer than you thought.

Claire's revised schedule for one week looked like this:

Monday	9.00a.m. to 5.00p.m. work
	6.00p.m. to 9.00p.m. meal, children
	9.00p.m. to 10.30p.m. preparatory reading for tomorrow's lecture
Tuesday	9.00a.m. to 5.00p.m. work
	6.00p.m. meal
	7.00p.m. to 9.00p.m. theology course
Wednesday	9.00a.m. to 5.00p.m. work
	6.00p.m. to 9.00p.m. meal, children
	9.00p.m. to 10.30p.m. follow up on last night's lecture
Thursday	10.00a.m. to 1.00p.m. choose essay title, initial ideas, library visit for books, an hour's reading
	afternoon washing and cleaning, time with children
	9.00p.m. to 10.30p.m. reading and notes for essay
Friday	10.00a.m. to 1.00.p.m. study, review notes to date, further reading
	afternoon weekly shop
	evening free time
Weekend	family, friends, home and church.

Take time to review the previous week's schedule before planning the next one, in order to learn from the previous week and to build in necessary adjustments. For example, is 9.00 to 10.30p.m. the best time to study, or might Claire try working for an hour early in the morning?

Analysing tasks and setting targets

Sometimes it is helpful to plan a number of weeks ahead in the same way that you plan ahead for holidays and celebrations. When you do this, it might be a good idea to sketch in the tasks for future weeks without planning in detail. However, it is worth taking the time to plan the week ahead in detail because it helps you to make the most of the time available. We will begin by identifying some of the tasks related to any course and you may be able to add others:

• attending teaching sessions;
• reading through lecture notes;

- browsing in the library to find relevant books and articles;
- surfing the net to find relevant articles;
- reading up on a topic before a lecture;
- further reading on a topic to clarify a lecture;
- reading and making notes for essays;
- writing essays;
- discussing essay topics and study problems with fellow students/ tutors.

It is possible to identify three regular tasks related to particular times. These are *preparatory tasks* for the next session, *follow-up tasks* from the previous session and the *completion of the formal assessment*. In terms of priorities, the formal assessment is the most important (in an assessed course) and in an emergency the other two may be neglected in order to concentrate on this. We will consider preparatory and follow-up tasks in more detail now; formal assessments will be discussed in chapter 5.

Preparatory tasks These may have been set out very clearly in a course handbook, in which case the tasks are clear and it is relatively easy to allocate the appropriate time to them. Even then it takes practice to know how long a task will take to accomplish and it becomes a further skill of learning to give the right amount of time to any task in order to help to keep attention focused. For example, suppose that you are asked to study a Bible passage of 10–15 verses, using two or three commentaries, and to make notes. You will probably find that this takes a surprisingly long time (2–3 hours) because the study is detailed and every sentence, and sometimes every word, is significant. By contrast, if you have not been asked to prepare anything in particular, but you see that the next lecture is on baptism, for example, you may read a chapter of a book on baptism, which may take you no longer than half an hour. If, however, you were preparing to write an essay on baptism, your reading would be more thorough and involve you in making notes, which takes much more time. It may also be the case that you know quite a lot about baptism, so that part of your preparation might be to think about what you already know, write it down and give it a logical structure. By contrast, you might find later in this imaginary course (on Worship and Liturgy) that there is a lecture on 'The Divine Office'. Perhaps you are not sure what this means, in which case part of your preparation will be to find out.

Follow-up tasks The question of follow-up study for teaching sessions is related to issues of time, interest and assessment. Those who are really interested in every topic and have plenty of time at their disposal may read all the recommended books. Most people find that they need to select what should be followed up and their choice often relates to assessment requirements of the course (see chapter 5). Another particular task of follow-up study is to clarify teaching that has not been (fully) understood. There are at least three ways in which this may be done: to ask questions of the tutor during or after the teaching session; to read relevant books; to meet with fellow students and discuss the subject with them. Of course, it is possible to anticipate problems of this kind, especially when a subject is new to you, by undertaking preparatory reading. It may be helpful to allow more time for follow-up reading at the beginning of a course when the material may be unfamiliar to you.

Further reading

Baxter, R (1995), *Studying Successfully*, Aldbrough, St John Publications (part 2, section 16).

Bourner, T and Race, P (1990), *How to Win as a Part-Time Student*, London, Kogan Page (chapters 1–6).

Chambers, E and Northedge, A (1997), *The Arts Good Study Guide*, Milton Keynes, Open University (chapter 1).

Race, P (1992), *500 Tips for Students*, Oxford, Blackwell.

Williams, K (1989), *Study Skills*, London, Macmillan (pp. 50–63).

2. ASSEMBLING THE TOOLS

Introduction

In this chapter we identify a range of different resources and consider how they may be used to support the task of learning, for example, Bible dictionaries and theological dictionaries for basic information and an overview of a topic. We examine basic aids to reading an academic text, for example, use of the contents page and index. We conclude by examining the skills of skim-reading a book, using introductions to chapters and closing summaries.

The traditional resources for formal learning are books, journals and tutors. In most courses they still provide the basic means for learning. They have been supplemented by the use of visits, videos and the Internet. We will consider each of these in turn.

Reflecting on experience
Identify and assess the strengths and weaknesses of your personal theological library.

Make a note of what you already know about the theological resources offered by local bookshops and public and academic libraries. If your knowledge is limited, you will find it helpful to do further research.

If you were asked to research the meaning of the biblical word 'covenant', how would you set about the task? Compare your answer with the suggestions in this chapter.

Books

You will often be given a bibliography with your course outline and additional books may be recommended in teaching sessions. It is advisable to find a good bookshop that stocks a range of theology books and has a good record for quick delivery of book orders. Of course, access to an academic library is also important. If you have registered with a higher education institution for your course you will have access to the library. On your first visit there may be a guided tour, a video guide or a virtual tour to help you to find your way around and to get to know what services are offered. Also, libraries often have written guides freely available.

You may find that your application to join a library takes a week or more to process, but you can usually still use the books in the library without having borrowing rights. It is useful and enjoyable to browse the shelves designated for theology. If the library follows the Dewey system (and most do) you will find all theology books in the section numbered from 200–299. Another useful exercise is to familiarise yourself with the library catalogue. Many, but not all, of these are electronic, and are very simple to use. Most catalogues (electronic or paper based) are organised for searches under one of the following headings: author (surname followed by first name or initial), title or subject. Each book has a catalogue number on the (Dewey) system and is shelved with others on a similar subject. Thus, if you know one book in the library that you need, you will find others on the same theme shelved next to it; or alternatively you can use the subject catalogue to find all the books on a particular theme. If the book that you need has already been borrowed, you may want to enquire about the library's recall system. As long as you are preparing well in advance for writing an essay, you should be able to recall a book within about three weeks.

There are a number of different kinds of important books for studying theology, many of which may already be familiar to you. They include: theological and Bible dictionaries and encyclopedias of various kinds, Bible concordances, Bible commentaries and sourcebooks of documents and introductory readers. In a library some of them will be in the reference section and others on the open shelves; the library catalogue should enable you to locate them.

Some general points can be made before considering each kind in turn. Theological and Bible dictionaries sometimes bear the name of the publisher, for example, *The Eerdman's Bible Dictionary* (Myers, 1987). They may also be linked to a learned society or to a particular church, for example, *Harper's Bible Commentary* (Mays, 1988), which was written in association with the Society of Biblical Literature, and *The New Jerome Biblical Commentary* (Brown, Fitzmyer and Murphy, 1991), which was written by 'English-speaking Catholic exegetes' (biblical commentators), working in the spirit of Vatican II.

Not only do different works originate from different churches and publishers, but these also indicate different theological standpoints. For example, dictionaries and commentaries published by IVP are theologically and biblically evangelical and conservative, whereas similar publications from SCM and Harper will usually be more liberal. It is important in your studies, whatever your own theological roots, that you engage as openly as possible with those of different traditions. It is in this way that you will gain a better understanding of why people hold views that are different from your own.

There are a number of other aids for studying the Bible. A Bible concordance identifies different passages in which the same word occurs. There are different concordances for different versions of the Bible and works of different detail. Two of the classics remain *Young's Analytical Concordance to the Holy Bible*, based on the *Authorised Version* and *Cruden's Concordance* available in a number of different versions. Concordances are useful for thematic work based in one or more books of the Bible. For example, suppose you are doing a study of different New Testament metaphors of the church, you might wish to find all the New Testament references to the 'body' or to the 'household' and so on. Looking up these words in the concordance would provide you with most, if not all, of the relevant references.

Another important biblical reference book is a Bible dictionary. One attractive three-volume colour version is the *New Bible Dictionary* (Douglas, 1965) from IVP. It is traditional and conservative in outlook. More recently IVP has begun to publish more specialised dictionaries, for example a *Dictionary of Jesus and the Gospels* (Green, McKnight and Marshall, 1992) and a *Dictionary of Paul and His Letters* (Hawthorne, Martin and Reid, 1993). Such volumes make available the best of evangelical scholarship. The most recent publication on a larger scale than any previous work is the *Anchor Bible Dictionary*, accessible on CD-ROM, which should be available in most libraries of higher education institutions. Another type of book rather like a dictionary is a companion to the Bible. Recommended ones would be *The Oxford Companion to the Bible* (Metzger, 1993) and *The Cambridge Companion to Biblical Interpretation* (Barton, 1998).

The key remaining biblical reference tool is the commentary. This provides an introduction to the biblical books, articles on issues like the authority of the Bible, biblical criticism and biblical theology and a verse-by-verse comment on the whole text. There are some excellent one-volume Bible commentaries which give an overview and helpful summaries of every passage in every biblical book. Mention has already been made of two excellent commentaries of this kind, *The New Jerome Biblical Commentary* and *Harper's Bible Commentary*. Different publishers such as Word, A and C Black and Cambridge University Press (and many others) also produce whole series of individual commentaries on the Old and New Testaments. The key purpose of these is to provide an overview of each passage, drawing attention to key issues, followed by a detailed exegesis (a verse-by-verse analysis) of the text. They may also include articles on authorship, date and key themes of the biblical book. Finally, mention should be made of the excellent series of short Old Testament Guides and New Testament Guides, published by Sheffield Academic Press, which discuss themes and issues and present a summary of the most up-to-date scholarship. The intention is to provide one for every biblical book. Good examples of these series are provided by the guides on *1 and 2 Samuel* (Gordon, 1998) and *1 Corinthians* (Dunn, 1995). See also *A Dictionary of Biblical Interpretation* (Coggins and Houlden, 1990).

Just as there is a variety of reference works on the Bible, so there is a variety on different aspects of theology. We might begin by noting general dictionaries and encyclopedias of theology such as *A New Dictionary of Christian Theology* (Richardson and Bowden, 1983); *The New Dictionary of Theology* (Komonchak, 1987) and *The Blackwell Encyclopedia of Modern Christian Thought* (McGrath, 1993). Recently, more specialised theological dictionaries have been published, such as *An A to Z of Feminist Theology* (Isherwood and McEwan, 1996). Two standard dictionaries of the Christian church are Cross and Livingstone (1997) and Douglas (1978).

Another important development has been the provision of sourcebooks or readers, which provide extracts on important doctrines from the writings of key theologians throughout history, for example, *The Christian Theology Reader* (McGrath, 1995); *Readings in Christian Theology* (Hodgson and King, 1985). As in biblical studies, there are also introductory works which give an overview of Christian theology in its historical context, for example, *Christian Theology: an introduction* (McGrath, 1994); *Christian Theology: an introduction to its traditions and tasks* (Hodgson and King, 1994).

Other subjects, such as ethics, liturgy and pastoral theology, which form a significant part of courses in theological education and ministry, have similarly been resourced by dictionaries. These include, for example, *A New Dictionary of Christian Ethics* (Childress, 1986); *A New Dictionary of Liturgy and Worship* (Davies, 1986); *A Dictionary of Ethics, Theology and Society* (Clarke, 1996); *The Blackwell Reader in Pastoral Theology* (Woodward, 1998); *Dictionary of Christian Ethics and Pastoral Theology* (Atkinson and Field, 1995). The production of new dictionaries and the revision of older ones is a continuing process, so it is important to use the library catalogue and to browse the shelves to check that you have the most recent revisions and publications.

Finally, there are other reference works which range across the broad spectrum of religion, for example, *The Encyclopedia of Religion* (Eliade, 1987) is in sixteen volumes and includes articles about all faiths. It is a monumental and extremely useful work, significant for a multi-cultural society like our own. For example, under the heading 'Worship' there are separate sections for the worship of all the major world faiths. An important older work is Hastings' *Encyclopedia of Religion and Ethics* (1908).

Journals

There are an enormous number of academic journals for theology covering subjects like biblical studies, Old Testament, New Testament, theology, feminist theology, ethics and church history. Some of the advantages of journals are that they give access to the most recent studies in a subject and they are sharply focused on specific topics. Their disadvantages are that many of them require advanced understanding of a subject. However, some are more readily accessible; for example, you might try *The Expository Times*, which has articles on biblical studies, theology, ethics and preaching, or *The British Journal of Theological Education*, which covers a range of subjects in theological education. They hold out the hope of providing you with an article closely related to the particular topic that you are studying. Any academic library should be able to provide you with a list of available journals. Back copies are usually catalogued in alphabetical order of journal title.

There is a multiplicity of journals on many different aspects of theology. The problem in the past was locating the relevant articles, which was a long-winded task. Sometimes all the articles in a volume of a journal have a related theme, and at other times they are totally unrelated. Thankfully, nowadays the Religions Index CD-ROM allows articles relevant to a topic to be more easily tracked down. It is even possible to programme the software so that it identifies only the articles in journals stocked by your particular library. This eliminates one of the greatest frustrations of the Religions Index, which is finding a long list of possible resources and then finding that none of them is stocked by your library. It may be helpful to know that, if sufficient time is available, academic libraries will obtain copies of articles for you from other libraries, for which there is a charge.

Tutors and students

In many cases information may be provided more quickly and comprehensively through information and communication technology (ICT). Tutors should not simply be regarded as a source of information. They are, arguably, far more important as sounding boards and models of how to argue a case and how to think critically. They are encouragers and guides, skilled in helping you to organise, relate and evaluate information, and challengers of unsubstantiated opinions. Fellow students are equally a resource for one another in working collaboratively by discussing lectures, preparing seminars together, sharing books and generally supporting one another.

Tutors are not always 'used' to the best effect by students, who sometimes regard them as a kind of 'knowledge-dispensing machine' which lasts for the duration of the teaching session. The effect of this is that when tutors ask whether they have been understood or whether there are any questions, they are often met with silence. Sometimes students are reticent about asking questions in front of a large group, but tutors are usually glad to answer individual questions at the end of a session. They will often give tutorials to advise on essay plans or to give feedback on marked essays. The best way to get the most from a tutor is to prepare beforehand, so that your questions are clear and specific. Although tutors are knowledgeable and skilled, it is also important to recognise the role of fellow students as a significant resource. One of the most enjoyable aspects of study is sharing ideas, knowledge, hopes and fears with fellow students. (See chapter 9 for further discussion of this theme.)

Visits

Visits can help to make study come alive. For example, you might visit different places of worship, either as a participant observer in a service or to study the varied setting of worship and symbolism. You might visit the British Museum or Trinity College, Dublin to view ancient manuscripts. Study tours of Greece and Turkey would enable you to trace the steps of St Paul and a visit to Israel would bring to life the Old and New Testaments, as well as allowing you to experience the meeting of three living faiths. Equally, fieldwork in the global South throws new light on Christianity, ethics, development and other faiths.

One of the ways of making the most of visits is to do some preparatory reading before you go and to make time for reflection while you are there, or immediately following the visit. Photographs obviously help you to recall a visit, but a learning journal can be used to record not only what you did but also the difference between your expectations and your actual experience, and how your understanding or you yourself were changed by it.

TV and videos

Learning is enhanced and supplemented by materials from television and video. Their advantages are numerous: you can study in the comfort of your own home, replay points that are more difficult to understand and listen to experts in the discipline. A wide variety of programmes can be relevant, for example, those related to Christian beliefs and practice, ministry and ethics, the church and politics, dialogue with other faiths and interpreting the Bible. Examples of such programmes include those from the Open University and series like *Everyman*. Sometimes video clips from films provide opportunities for learning, although a critical evaluation of their approach and presentation is vital. Academic libraries increasingly stock video study materials, as do the various religious education resources centres.

One of the good things about television and video is the stimulation to learning that they provide. However, one of their weaknesses is that they encourage uncritical responses, because most programmes by their very nature as entertainment are partisan, and different views from the one presented are seldom considered in the same programme. It can, therefore, be helpful to arrange to see a programme with a group of fellow students and to follow it with a discussion, in order to elicit a more critical perspective.

The Internet

For some people the Internet is second nature, for others it presents the challenge of the unknown. In fact the Internet is just another tool (and an increasingly significant one) for study. The Internet (or International Network) is a vast, global network of computers. Its rather lofty overall purpose is to create an encyclopedia of everything known by humankind and to help to create a worldwide learning community! Using the Internet provides many opportunities to support and extend your studies. One dimension of the Internet is the World Wide Web (WWW). The World Wide Web functions as an electronic encyclopedia or database which is growing constantly, so there is always more information being made available. Universities and colleges often have their own 'website' which may give access to their library catalogues and other online reference resources. Another dimension of the Internet is e-mail (electronic mail), which not only enables you to contact tutors and fellow students but also to join electronic discussion groups on virtually any subject.

The Internet is easy to use. Access is gained through an Internet provider such as BT or Global (or many others). You then need some useful addresses to begin searching for the information you require, with the help of search sites that will find locations referring to particular subjects. You can, of course, simply 'surf the net'. You may discover some wonderful information, but the activity is time-consuming. To some extent, the net's usefulness may depend on what you want to find, but it provides a wealth of information which is available to anyone who is willing to search for it. It is also worth noting that the quality of the information available varies considerably, so it should not be used indiscriminately.

Once you have linked onto the Internet the software is very user-friendly; for example, there is a back button to return to the previous page and an electronic bookmark facility in order to go straight to pages you have visited before. As you become used to it, you will gain in confidence.

EXERCISE

A helpful place to begin for resources for biblical studies is the appropriately named *Resource Pages for Biblical Studies*. Go to the site with the following address:

http://www.hivolda.no/asf/kkf/rel-stud.html

Make sure you have typed everything exactly as you see it, matching the case of the letters as well, before you press the return button.

Under PAGE 1 click <u>Bible Texts and Translations</u>
Under Translations, click <u>Bible Browser</u>
At the <u>Bible Browser</u> site, in the FETCH box type Adam.
Under WHAT ARE WE FETCHING, click WORD.
Under VERSION, click RSV.
Under CORPUS, click TaNaKh, or Old Testament.
Click RETRIEVE at the top of the page.

Answer the following:
How many times does 'Adam' occur in the Old Testament?

Use the 'back' button to make your way back to the Resources site (or retype the address). Spend a few minutes exploring this site. You may find something that is relevant for your current work!

Useful addresses

Here are some useful addresses for general search sites, issues concerned with theology and biblical studies and places to buy new and second-hand books. Within each section the addresses are listed alphabetically. There are, of course, thousands of other sites including virtual tours of sacred sites. Many local churches as well as cathedrals also have their own 'home page' where you can learn about history, services and their latest news.

Search sites

http://www.altavista.digital.com/ **AltaVista** – meant to be the largest general database

http://www.metacrawler.com/ **Metacrawler** – searches ten engines (databases) for you and gets the results http://www.yahoo.com/ **Yahoo** – good for giving organised results by subject category

Theology and biblical studies

http://lcweb.loc.gov/catalog/ **American Library of Congress**

http://atla.library.vanderbilt.edu/atla/refdesk/atlarefr.html **ATLA** – a help/tutorial site for the religious indexes on CD-ROM

http://www.bsw.org/ **Biblical Studies on the Web** – helpful links to available articles, study tools and so forth

http://ccel.wheaton.edu/ **Christian Classics Ethereal Library** – extensive collection of classics from Augustine to Wesley; though mostly old translations

http://www.goshen.net/ **Goshen Christian Search Engine** – contains interesting web links and study tools

http://www.csbsju.edu/library/Internet/theosubj.html **Internet Theology Resources** – exhaustive links across most theological subjects

http://www.sni.net/advent/ **New Advent Catholic Supersite** – church fathers, *Catholic Encyclopedia, Summa Theologica*

http://ccat.sas.upenn.edu/~humm/Resources/Texts/index.html **Online texts related to biblical study** – an extensive list of primary sources and web links

http://www.hivolda.no/asf/kkf/rel-stud.html **Resource Pages for Biblical Studies** – THE place to start for linked resources

http://www.ocf.org/OrthodoxPage/reading/St.Pachomius/Welcome.html **St Pachomius Library** – of early church fathers; well resourced

http://scholar.cc.emory.edu/ **Scholars Press website** – some very useful links, especially for biblical studies but also for theology

http://www.vatican.va/ **The Holy See** – the official Vatican site; interesting links and resources

http://www.knight.org/advent/summa/summa.htm **Thomas Aquinas'** full *Summa Theologica*

Books

http://www.amazon.com/ **Amazon Com** – THE best place to buy books on the net, and even to do research by subject category

http://www.bibliofind.com/ **Bibliofind** – a useful second-hand site, especially for theology

http://www.bookpages.co.uk/ **Book Pages UK** – UK equivalent of Bibliofind, though only for books in print

http://www.robibrad.demon.co.uk/Books.htm **Online Publishers and**

Booksellers – a site for links to buying TRS-related books, mostly Christian.

Basic aids to reading an academic text

On nearly all occasions when an essay is set for some form of assessment, a bibliography of recommended texts is given. It is always advisable to begin with these books and to use at least some of them. However, it often happens that not all of them are available and it becomes necessary to find others to replace them. We have already noted that books are catalogued in a way that sets those on the same theme alongside one another.

Having found the relevant section on the library shelves, imagine that you do not find the particular book on the bibliography for which you are searching, but you do notice others with similar titles. What should you do? First, you need to be aware that some titles are an actual reflection of their contents and some are not, so you need even at this stage to make a more thorough check. Next, you should read the contents pages in relation to the task that you have been set; does the book include a chapter or section of a chapter on that topic? If not, it may be helpful to turn to the back of the book and search the index or indices. These may include indices of names, biblical texts and, most important for your purpose, subjects, together with the relevant page numbers. If you turn to the relevant chapters from the list of contents or the appropriate page from the index, you will be able to glance through the relevant passages while you are in the library and make an informed judgement about whether the book will be useful. You may of course still find, when you get the book home, that it is not as useful as you thought it would be, but at least the method enables you to be more discerning than simply picking likely titles from the shelves.

Another thing to check is the publication date. There are classic works published earlier in the twentieth century, but books published within the last ten years should include the most recent scholarship. Finally, it is helpful to read the cover sleeve or back cover of the book, which usually gives details about the author and an abstract (explanation of the contents and purpose) of the book. It is sometimes possible to tell from this information whether the setting of the book is American or British scholarship, whether the theological perspective is Roman Catholic, Anglican or Protestant, and liberal or conservative. Remember that our view is that an informed balance of a range of views helps you to recognise, understand and engage significantly with theological issues.

It is often the case when beginning a new area of study that the technical vocabulary can seem formidable: 'eschatological', 'exegetical' and 'christological' can be very confusing. Authors of introductory texts increasingly help their readers by providing a glossary of relevant terms at the end of the book. Like learning any new language, it is vital to be confident about basic vocabulary. Here are three approaches that you might find helpful:

- find and use a text with a glossary for each discipline, for example, for biblical studies, for theology, for liturgy;
- use a dictionary on that subject, like the ones described earlier in this chapter (not an ordinary English dictionary), in order to give you a more detailed background;
- test your understanding by either explaining the concept to a friend or by making your own glossary.

Skim reading

The purpose of skim reading is to find out whether the material, usually a chapter of a book or an article, is relevant to your task. If you can plan the time, it is often helpful to select the books from the library shelves on the basis of titles, contents and indices, and then to settle down for an hour to skim read them to ensure that they are relevant to your purpose. This also acts as a stimulus to further reading. You cannot wait to get home to read 'the find' that is so relevant to your essay!

One method for skim reading a chapter of a book, or an article, is to focus on three sections: first, read the introduction or opening paragraph, which should explain the purpose, content and sequence of the chapter. Next, look through the chapter and identify the various subheadings in order to judge whether any or all are relevant to your task. Finally, read the conclusion or summary (usually the last paragraph of a chapter), which should confirm what has been said in the introduction.

EXERCISE
When you are given your next topic to research, or your next presentation or essay to prepare, try to put the method described into practice: ▶▶

- read the introduction of the chapter and note its purpose, content and order;
- note the headings of the different sections;
- read the conclusion, noting from the summary the content and argument of the chapter.

All of the above should be in sufficient agreement to give you a sense of the content and argument of the whole chapter.

Further reading

Baxter, R (1995), *Studying Successfully*, Aldbrough, St John Publications, (part 2, sections 17, 28 and 30).

Brown, R E, Fitzmyer, J A and Murphy, R E (eds) (1991), *The New Jerome Biblical Commentary*, London, Geoffrey Chapman.

Mays, J L (ed.) (1988), *Harper's Bible Commentary*, New York, Harper.

McGrath, A (ed.) (1993), *The Blackwell Encyclopedia of Modern Christian Thought*, Oxford, Blackwell.

Metzer, B (ed.) (1993), *The Oxford Companion to the Bible*, Oxford, Oxford University Press.

3. EFFECTIVE READING

Introduction

The aim of this chapter is to enable you to develop further your skills of deep reading in order to enhance learning.

It is broken down into four tasks. The chapter:

- examines deep or close reading and seeks to clarify its aims of understanding, selecting what is relevant and reading critically;
- explores methods of deep reading (highlighting, underlining, making notes) using an extract from an academic text;
- considers the importance of the skill of précis in clarifying the heart of an argument and suggests ways to develop the skill;
- considers the recognition and evaluation of bias or differing perspectives in authors.

Reflecting on experience

Think of two experiences of any kind of reading that you have done; one that you enjoyed, and the other that you disliked. Can you explain the reasons for the differences and consider how such experiences may relate to your studies?

Compare and contrast your experience of the different ways in which you read the following: a newspaper, a novel, *The Highway Code*, an academic theology textbook.

The nature and aims of deep reading

In the last chapter we considered the usefulness of skim reading as a means to discover the relevance of a book and to identify sections for further study. This chapter examines close or deep reading in order to absorb information, to understand new ideas and the ways in which these are combined to form various arguments.

This kind of reading is more difficult than reading a newspaper article or a novel, or *The Highway Code*. In a newspaper the articles are short, use a narrower range of vocabulary and have an immediate relevance. In a novel the narrative and characters help the reader to keep in touch with the story, and there may be whole sections of description which are not essential to the main plot. In the case of *The Highway Code*, the text is presented as a series of laws and good practice to be learned. However, in the case of academic reading, many books and articles include both a wide range of vocabulary, some of it technical and unfamiliar, and also closely reasoned argument which requires the reader's full and constant attention if the passage is to be understood.

We may find two kinds of new vocabulary in academic reading: one is technical and the other is related to the style of academic writing.

Technical vocabulary refers to the specialist vocabulary of the subject. It enables writers to be precise and concise and to share the same meaning of a word within the community of scholars. All areas of theology will share some technical vocabulary, for example, words like 'eschatology' meaning study of the last things, 'sub-apostolic' meaning the historical period after the apostles, 'hermeneutics' meaning interpretation. Specialist words like these are usually best researched in a theological or Bible dictionary. Additionally, however, different disciplines within theology, like systematic theology, biblical studies and church history, will have specialist vocabulary particular to their areas. For example, some vocabulary in biblical studies is either taken from or written in Greek or Hebrew. If you wish to pursue studies in this area in greater depth, it would be helpful at least to learn the alphabet and rudiments of grammar, in order to be able to read Greek and Hebrew words in academic texts and commentaries.

Academic vocabulary, which usually allows authors to write more succinctly, may range from unusual words with classical origins to words in German, and words newly created by the academic community, such as 'superordination' as the opposite of 'subordination'. They can usually be found in a good dictionary, such as *The Shorter Oxford English Dictionary* (in two volumes 1993) or *Chambers Concise Dictionary* (new edition 1991). Sometimes it is possible to guess at the meaning of a word from the context; sometimes it is necessary to stop reading and to look it up. Another feature of academic writing is the way in which authors tend to write fairly cautiously. They use words like 'may' or 'might' to introduce arguments and explain, sometimes at great length, the limitations or exceptions to the argument. Every argument that is advanced is supported by carefully selected evidence.

Programmes like *Mastermind* or *University Challenge* may seem to suggest that academic study is about learning more facts. It is true that we gain knowledge from learning, but in theology we are more often concerned with understanding new ideas and new ways of interpreting information, and with debating issues and asking questions. In order to be able to do this we need, in our reading, to understand both the argument that is being made and the evidence for it. This demands attentive reading and active intellectual engagement with what we read.

Methods of deep reading

In order to examine skills and methods of deep reading, we will analyse the reading of a typical piece of academic writing with some of the features that we have noted earlier. The chosen piece is an extract from a book in this series entitled *Using the Bible* (Evans, 1999). In order to do the analysis it is essential that you read the extract attentively, with active intellectual engagement, using whatever methods you normally use to help you to understand an academic text. For example, you may choose to underline, highlight or make brief notes in the margin. (We suggest that you photocopy the extract so that you can refer to it easily when reading subsequent pages of this book and so that you are also free to write on the photocopy.) The extract is about Bible stories for children.

> The first authors and editors of the books of the Bible almost certainly did not have an audience of children in mind. They are adult books, and the ancient cultures in many ways focused less on the development of children than we do today. The use of story to convey so much of the matter makes some parts of the Bible apparently accessible to young children as well as to adults. Is this really so?
>
> Story makes a great workshop and playground for the imagination, and imagination is surely essential in the development of religious understanding. Story-telling also leads to 'open-ended' interpretation where there is not one, closed, interpretation but different readers may take different meanings from a text. Should children be guided to one meaning or be allowed to make what they will of a biblical story?

Stories can offer children the opportunity to think about, and empathise with, characters. However, there are probably few biblical characters whose stories are really suitable for the world and understanding of a young child. Most collections of Bible stories for children are very selective about which stories are chosen and also very selective about what meaning is to be conveyed. For example, we may question whether the stories about Noah, David and even Jesus recorded in Genesis 9:18–25, 2 Samuel 11:2–5 and Luke 12:42–53, are suitable ones to read to children. (There is no shortage of sex and violence in scripture.)

The question of 'stages' of faith development in children has been studied and there are insights in this enquiry for how a child may interpret a story. Does it matter if a story is presented as 'true' or, like some folk and fairy stories, not entirely or not at all true? Do we present the story of Jonah and the big fish as a story or as history? Is that story to be treated differently from the story of an angel speaking to Mary (Luke 1), or of Jesus' resurrection (Matthew 28)?

The racial discrimination of Old Testament books in favour of Israel against the other inhabitants of Palestine (whose descendants share with Jews the land of Israel today) may be a prejudice we do not wish our children to practise. The anti-Jewish perspective in the Gospels also carries dangers and needs careful handling (and arguably this is no less true for adults than children).

Whenever a story is retold, with new words and out of the context in which it is set in the version in the Bible, a new meaning may emerge. Some of the versions of Bible stories for children do not seem to have the same theological message as the versions of these stories in the Bible. The many retellings for children of 'David and Goliath' tend to emphasise the character of the boy David. He is, moreover, often portrayed in the pictures accompanying the story as being of an age with the children for whom the story is targeted, though in the text he is a 'stripling' (1 Samuel 17:56), a young man rather than a boy. The result is often that the retold story seems to be about David's heroism, about courage and skill in the face of danger. While this is an element in the biblical narrative of 1 Samuel 17, it is probably secondary. David is not here the hero-soldier: that role belongs to Saul (or even Goliath). The main point, and the underlying theology, seems rather that human greatness counts as nothing, but victory comes through the might or grace of God. This is the message in David's speech in 1 Samuel 17:45–47: God can use even an instrument as unlikely and as unheroic as David to bring victory over Israel's enemies.

The suitability of this story for children, however told (see, for example, 1 Samuel 17:52–54), is another matter. It is worth reflecting on how far two of the stories most frequently retold for children differ from the stuff of video 'nasties': the wholesale destruction of life in the Great Flood (Genesis 6 to 9) and this slaughter of Goliath and the Philistines (1 Samuel 17).

EXERCISE

How would you describe the experience of reading the extract?

How long did it take you to read it?

What methods did you use to help yourself to understand what you were reading?

What is the extract about?

Summarise the author's argument.

List the difficulties, if any, that you experienced in studying the extract.

Having done this, you may like to compare your own response with the answers given to the above questions in turn by a student and then by one of the authors. First, these answers were given by a student, Vicki:

• I found it interesting and quite thought-provoking. I don't think I have ever seriously questioned the wisdom or otherwise of introducing children to Bible stories.

• It took me about six minutes to read; I would need to re-read it if I had to work with it.

• I did not make any notes, but I did have a pen in my hand. I always find it easier to think like this.

• The extract calls into question the introduction of Bible stories to children. It does not say that it is wrong but asks the reader to think about the issues involved, to weigh up the pros and cons.

• The Bible was written for adults. How far can children understand it?

A lot of selection is made by adults of suitable material, usually stories, but perhaps not with full regard to the implications, for example, gender and race issues, which would not be appropriate to explain at this level but would be left at face value. What do we want children to learn? Are stories biased towards one meaning only (depending on the thoughts of the editor)?
• No difficulties.

The answers given by Ruth Ackroyd were similar to those given by Vicki:
• I enjoyed reading the passage; I found it interesting and challenging to face the questions that Evans raises. I found the language and approach accessible and the short paragraphs indicated helpfully the changes of direction in the argument. Nevertheless, the reasoning behind the argument is tightly focused and the argument itself moves quickly, so that I had to concentrate fully in order to absorb all the points that were being made.
• The extract took me about eight minutes to read but, like Vicki, I would need to revisit it to check some of the details.
• I underlined the key points of the argument and core content in the text, and used letters and numbers to clarify the different parts of the argument. I reinforced my understanding by writing headings and brief explanations in the margin of the text.
• The extract is about the appropriateness of Bible stories for children. It raises in particular, problems of violence, children's perceptions of truth and issues of gender and racism.
• Evans argues that a number of biblical stories are not in fact appropriate for children, and that children's authors sometimes significantly alter the theological meaning of such stories in order to make them more accessible.
• I experienced no inherent difficulties in understanding the text, but I felt that I needed to make a few notes to help me to organise and absorb the different points being made.

There are a number of things to notice about these two responses as well as some further points to raise about the extract.

The experience of reading

The response to the first question was positive. It is usually easier to read about a subject which you find interesting. The experience of reading may also be related to other factors such as prior knowledge and the perceived relevance of the extract. Different types of academic writing assume different levels of knowledge or familiarity with the subject being explored. The extract given here has been written at an introductory level but, nevertheless, you may have found, for example, that the key idea, of the inappropriateness of many biblical stories for children, was new to you. In the case of more advanced reading, if you do not already possess sufficient prior knowledge to understand it, you may need to examine further some basic concepts by using Bible and theological dictionaries. The effect of this is to slow down your progress, but checking, for example, basic vocabulary pays dividends in subsequent understanding.

It is also the case that reading becomes increasingly significant when you can relate it either to previous learning or to a particular interest that you have, or to a task that needs to be completed. These factors increase motivation to read attentively. It is also difficult to enjoy reading if, unlike this extract, you have to stop at every other word to look up its meaning.

Reading and time management

The length of time that it takes to read an extract is related both to the difficulty of the extract and to the depth of reading being undertaken. Both readers quoted here found the extract relatively easy; it took them an average of seven minutes to read an 800-word extract. Both also said that they would need to revisit it in order to make notes if they were to use it in other work. It might be helpful in planning work schedules to know how long to allow yourself for reading a chapter of a book or an article. Based on this exercise, we might suggest that it would take about seven minutes to read an extract of 800 words, fifteen minutes to read and make notes on it. These suggestions are for guidance only but they may be helpful in setting goals, which are important when you are faced with a quantity of reading, as you are when you are studying.

Methods to aid understanding

Different people use different methods to help them to understand their reading. Some use a highlighter on their personal photocopy, to mark the main argument and the salient points in order to make it stand out from the rest of the text. An important point here is to be clear about your criteria for highlighting and to limit its use so that it does not lose its purpose amidst a sea of highlighted text! Other people make notes on the text of their own copy, commenting on whether or not they agree with the writer, and on the strength of the argument. All of these are strategies for active reading, helping you to focus on and engage with the text. If you are going to use your reading as a resource for your essay, then it is best to write separate notes.

Many students, and perhaps especially some older students, become so interested in everything they are reading that they forget the purpose for which they began to read and get sidetracked into fascinating but irrelevant detail. One of the ways of addressing this tendency is to bring to your reading the key question that you are seeking to address and to keep it in mind as you read. You may decide to write down the key question and to have it in view as you read and make notes.

Making notes

Notes usually identify and summarise the argument of the passage, before making a critical response to it. They order the reading into main and subsidiary points and will usually be adapted to answer the particular question that the reader brings to the text. For example, you may have been asked which Bible stories are most suitable for children. This passage does not answer that question directly but it does make some useful points which relate to that question. Ruth Ackroyd's notes were influenced by the fact that she thought that Evans had been rather negative towards the appropriateness of Bible stories for children. She, therefore, included some reflection on Bible stories that, taking into account Evans' concerns, she felt might still be appropriate and important for children. Her notes were set out like this:

> **Key point:** Many Bible stories are inappropriate for, and their meanings are inaccessible, to children.
> * The stories were written for adults rather than children; such was the culture in Old Testament and New Testament times.
> * Stories about some of the famous biblical characters, for example, David and Noah, are inappropriate for children because they contain violence and sex.
> * Children have a limited capacity to understand the difference between various kinds of truth (literal and metaphorical) and to distinguish between various kinds of writing.
>
> **Key point:** Care must be exercised when choosing Bible stories for children. Selections must take account of the need to:

- explain the historical context appropriately for children;
- balance the number of stories told about men and women;
- handle racial perspectives sensitively;
- identify the appropriate theological message of the story for children.

A critical response: Notwithstanding Evans' argument, there are some stories that are appropriate and accessible for children, for example, many of the parables of Jesus, such as 'The Lost Sheep' and 'The Friend at Midnight', and also the story of the life of Jesus. According to the Gospel accounts there were children among the crowds who listened to Jesus, and presumably they enjoyed his stories.

There may be a case, as with other types of children's stories, for giving edited highlights which are appropriate in subject matter and for ease of understanding.

Difficulties experienced in reading the extract

In the extract given here, no particular difficulties were evident by the two readers because the writer, in order to make the work accessible, had deliberately avoided the use of technical language and long paragraphs.

The skill of précis

To précis means to summarise. The summary may be of a paragraph, a chapter in a book or a whole book. In each case the aim is the same: to identify and state the heart of the argument in your own words. The method for doing this involves identifying the subject of the passage and the argument being put forward in connection with it, then stripping away material that is not central to the argument. This would include examples and evidence used to support the main argument. Very often the argument is repeated in different ways. Sometimes a counter-argument is mentioned and rejected, and the accepted argument is clarified in opposition to the rejected argument. Having identified the main argument, the subsidiary points are then re-assembled in your own words.

To be able to summarise the argument demonstrates that you have understood the passage, but usually more is required of your reading than this.

Recognising and evaluating differing perspectives

Christians approach their theological studies from within particular Christian traditions. This is also true of authors of theological texts; many, but not all, writers in the area write from within the Christian tradition and sometimes from within a particular branch of that tradition. Some authors may be related to a particular Christian church or branch of Protestantism or Catholicism, or to a particular theological perspective, for example, conservative, traditional, liberal or radical. It is important to understand that authors and students alike arrive at a particular perspective as a result of complex factors such as upbringing, or personal choice based on critical reflection. In most cases perspectives are not fixed for life and students change their perspectives in response to new understanding, experience and critical reflection.

One of the prerequisites of effective reading is to be both open to and academically critical of new or different ideas and arguments which may appear to threaten our established perspective. It is important to realise that the fact that someone holds a different perspective does not negate the argument that they are making; only evidence can do that! If you fundamentally disagree with what you are reading, the challenge to you is to find the evidence to demonstrate that your viewpoint is valid and reasonable. Sometimes we simply have to acknowledge that different people may interpret the same evidence in different ways.

Further reading

Baxter, R (1995), *Studying Successfully*, Aldbrough, St John Publications (part 2, section 17).

Chambers, E and Northedge, A (1997), *The Arts Good Study Guide*, Milton Keynes, Open University Press.

Fairbairn, G J and Winch, C (1991), *Reading, Writing and Reasoning: a guide for students*, Milton Keynes, SRHE and Open University Press (pp. 7–22).

4. EFFECTIVE WRITING

Introduction

One of the fundamental forms of assessment in higher education is essay-writing. Some people seem to be able to write good essays with no apparent effort, while others really have to struggle to present a polished piece of writing. It is the view of the authors of this book that it is possible to develop the necessary skills of essay-writing and the object of this chapter is to help with that task.

In this chapter we will:

- consider the characteristics of a good essay;
- examine one particular approach to essay-writing, using a typical essay title;
- analyse some examples of essay-writing;
- explain the mechanics of referencing and presenting bibliographies.

Reflecting on experience
When did you last write an essay?

Can you remember any advice that you were given at that time or any strategies that you used which were helpful?

What process do you think you might follow in preparing to write and in writing an essay?

The characteristics of a good essay

Good essays share a number of characteristics. We will list these and then examine each in turn. A good essay:

- has a helpful title;
- has an introduction, development and conclusion;
- addresses the title throughout;
- is held together by a clear argument;
- is structured in paragraphs which develop the argument and provide supporting evidence;
- is well written.

A helpful title

This may seem a strange place to begin because on many occasions you are given an essay title or, preferably, a number of titles from which to choose. However, you may be encouraged to make up your own essay title. A good title will help you to write a good essay. Your title should make your task clear, specific and feasible and encourage you to construct an argument that hangs together. One way of designing your own title is to choose a topic within the course that really interests you; then you may need to focus it more sharply to make the subject manageable in a limited number of words. You may then begin to address specific questions to this area. As you make your selection of the best question, you edit it until it meets the criteria given here.

To take an example: you are studying Paul's letters and you are particularly interested in Colossians. You want to know whether some members of the church in Colossae held beliefs with which Paul did not agree and, if so, what the nature and origin of these beliefs were. You might begin with 'Was there a Colossian heresy and, if so, what was its nature and origin?' This might be refined to, 'To what extent is it accurate to speak of a Colossian heresy?'

Even if you do not choose your own title, but select one from the options given, there are two fairly obvious checks to be made. First, if at all possible choose a title on a subject that interests you. In academic study, as in life generally, it is the case that sometimes you have to work at things that do not interest you, but it is much easier to motivate yourself to work on something that you enjoy. Second, ensure that you know that you understand the title. We will examine this further under 'Addressing the title' but it is relevant to say at this stage that, when choosing a title, students sometimes select a subject because they understand what they have to do, even though the subject may not really interest them, rather than selecting a more difficult title related to an interesting subject. To 'play safe' in this way in an examination is understandable and sensible, but in choosing an essay title it might be wiser to spend time analysing the title.

An introduction, development and conclusion

An old adage for writing essays is that in the introduction you say what you intend to do; in the body of the essay, you do it; in the conclusion you say what you have done. Such advice includes some necessary elements but omits others. For example, students sometimes launch straight into the first point that they wish to make rather than opening up their subject and setting out their argument and way of working. In the body of the essay some students seem to forget what, in the introduction, they gave as an outline of what they were going to do, and wander away from both subject and argument. Sometimes, particularly when students have run over their word limit or are pressed for time, they omit the conclusion entirely and finish instead on the last point of the body of the essay. A good conclusion should summarise the argument that has been constructed in the essay to answer the question.

Presenting a coherent argument

Addressing the title throughout the essay is akin to bearing in mind the relevant question(s) as you read a text book. A good essay makes reference to the title, subject and argument, frequently and explicitly, using a variety of vocabulary.

One way of envisaging a coherent argument is to imagine it as a corridor with doors leading from it. The various doors represent different stages in the argument. It is necessary in moving along the corridor to proceed through each door in turn in order to explore the room beyond, but equally it is necessary to return through the door to the corridor before moving on to the next door. (There are no connecting doors between rooms in this establishment that would allow you to wander through rooms at will!) In the same way the writer has a clear and focused argument in mind. Each point in the argument is explored separately and firmly related to the main argument, before moving on to the next point. Another way of imagining a coherent argument is as a thread. When someone is explaining to us their ideas for an essay or their reasons for doing something, we sometimes say, 'I have lost the thread of your argument', meaning that the link between two ideas or reasons is unclear. It is important when writing an essay that the thread of the argument is clear and unbroken.

Nevertheless the argument will no doubt include related and

opposing arguments and contrasts. These may be signalled by changes in paragraph and also by trigger words such as 'however', 'nevertheless', 'another' or 'additionally', and so on.

Paragraphs

An essay is structured in individual paragraphs, each of which develops the argument by exploring one main point or section of the argument. This may helpfully be expressed in the opening sentence. The rest of the paragraph then develops or explains the argument, supported by appropriate evidence, examples and citation of authorities. If you find that a paragraph is particularly long, you may find it helpful to check whether you have tried to handle too many points in it. Sometimes, if an argument is complex, it may achieve greater clarity if you break it up into shorter paragraphs. In a similar way, the meaning of long sentences may also be clarified by reworking them into shorter ones. Not all paragraphs have to be the same length: a short one, carrying a fundamental argument, can be very effective.

A well-written essay

A well-written essay is one that is easy to read, is grammatically accurate, is without awkward phrases and does not contain spelling errors. These qualities are achieved naturally by some people and by painstaking revision and editing by others. There are a number of ways to help yourself with this task. You may read through the essay, identifying and correcting expressions which are imprecise or clumsy. You may achieve the same purpose by reading the essay out loud, or asking a fellow student to read it. You may find a thesaurus and a dictionary helpful in extending your vocabulary and range of expression. Further assistance can be gained from computer software, which identifies poor expression and incorrect spelling. There are some basic rules for formal essay-writing, such as: do not abbreviate 'it is' to 'it's'; do not, in a list of examples, write 'etc.' or even 'et cetera' (it will look as though either you could not think of other examples, or you could not be bothered to include them).

Students are often unsure about whether to write in the third person or the first person, especially when they are urged to include their own views. The traditional answer, still found in many textbooks on the subject, is that one should write in the third person in order to focus attention on what is being written rather than on the person writing. It is, of course, still possible, using this method, to include one's own argument and critical assessment of the evidence. For example, instead of writing,

'I think that Ackroyd is wrong in citing infant baptism as a significant characteristic of the Anglican church', one could write, 'There are several weaknesses in Ackroyd's view that infant baptism is a significant characteristic of the Anglican church.'

It is equally true that many authors today do write in the first person, either as 'I' or 'we'. At least three reasons lie behind this. One is the influence of experiential learning on academic writing. It is increasingly common to include critical reflection on personal experience as legitimate evidence to support an argument. A second reason for writing in the first person is to emphasise the process of interaction and dialogue between author and reader in the process of reading. It is then an attempt to engage the reader in active reading. Third, writing in the first person stresses the 'ownership' of what is being said.

Inclusive language and God language

The issues of inclusive language and language for God are sensitive ones. Let us take inclusive language first and assume that however we express ourselves, we consider it right to be inclusive of all people. Some people are of the view that 'man' is a generic as well as a gendered word and includes women as well as men. Other people argue that 'man' excludes women because it has to stand both for men and as a generic word. It therefore seems to be preferable to use words other than 'man' when describing both men and women, for example, words like 'humankind', 'people', and 'persons'.

Singular pronouns 'he' and 'she' can be a particular problem. Some people solve it by writing s/he; others try to write in the plural. You can find examples of attempts to write inclusively if you compare the *Revised Standard Version* of the Bible with the *New Revised Standard Version* and also if you compare the liturgies in the Anglican *Alternative Service Book 1980* with the suggested changes in the book *Making Women Visible* (General Synod Liturgical Commission, 1989).

Language about God is, if anything, an even more sensitive question. Christians agree that God is not gendered, that is to say that God is neither male nor female. If this is the case, how then should we write about God? Traditionally Christians have referred to God as 'He', largely because of the Christian understanding of God as 'Father', which is not, of course, affected by this discussion. One way forward is to consistently replace sentences in which God is referred to as 'He' with 'God'. Similarly, instead of writing 'His', you would write 'God's'. This can make for awkward sentences if the word 'God/God's' crops up repeatedly, but careful rewording can avoid this problem.

An approach to essay-writing

There is no one correct approach to essay-writing, although there are characteristics that an essay should have, which have been outlined in the previous section. How you actually achieve those characteristics in your essay is a matter of your own approach and choices. If you have a method that works well for you and achieves the necessary results, there is no need to change it. However, if you are new to essay-writing or are finding it difficult to know how to set about the task, you may find the approach recommended in the next few pages helpful.

We begin with an overview of the task. The stages of writing an essay include:

- addressing the title;
- finding appropriate resources and making useful notes;
- clarifying your argument and planning the essay;
- writing and editing the essay;
- checking references and adding a bibliography.

Addressing the title

We will take as an example an essay title that was set for a diocesan course and examine its different parts. We shall follow a process of setting you a number of exercises related to the essay and then we shall comment on each exercise. The essay title is: *What are the significant characteristics of your own denomination and what are its strengths and weaknesses?*

EXERCISE
Identify and write down the subject of the essay. Compare your findings with ours.

We think that the subject of the essay is *your own denomination*. If this is the case then to write either about another denomination, or another subject like preaching, would strictly speaking be irrelevant. You might mention them as part of your answer, for example to draw a contrast, or as one of the characteristics, strengths or weaknesses of your denomination, but you must only do so for a good reason.

The subject, *your own denomination*, appears to introduce a personal faith dimension into the essay, which is rare in theoretical academic writing but which has always been relevant in training for a variety of ministries within the churches. The title seems to suggest that someone who did not belong to a denomination would not be able to answer the question. In fact, a slight change of phrase to 'a particular denomination' would make it possible for anyone to attempt an answer. Nevertheless, the original version of the title suggests personal engagement with the question, which should not, however, lead merely to the iteration of personal opinion.

EXERCISE
Write down the aspects or areas of the subject that you are asked to consider, and explain what they mean. Compare your findings with ours.

There are two aspects to consider: *the significant characteristics* of your own denomination and *its strengths and weaknesses*. Let us look at each of these in a little more detail.

The word 'characteristics' refers to the typical qualities or traits of the chosen denomination. The inclusion of the adjective 'significant' requires the writer to select from all the possible characteristics the ones that are the most important, valuable and distinctive.

'Strengths and weaknesses' as concepts are self-explanatory, but their identification forms what is in fact the critical or evaluative section of the essay because you will have to make judgements about what those strengths and weaknesses are and, of course, support your judgements with evidence. For example, your experience may tell you that one of the weaknesses of your denomination is long and boring sermons, but you have only your own experience (and perhaps the anecdotal evidence of your friends) to support you. Such experience is insufficient evidence, and rather too personal to form a judgement. Of course, you might want to conduct a questionnaire in your deanery to test this perception. At this stage you are moving from personal opinion to seeking evidence from fieldwork to test your view.

Most essay titles are constructed in such a way that they provide a clear directive about what to do in relation to the subject which is to be considered. The directive is usually a verb and is often called a trigger. Examples of such triggers are: 'discuss', 'evaluate', 'assess', 'explain', 'identify', 'comment on'. Triggers usually occur at the beginning of the title but on some occasions, for example, where a quotation is used as part of a title, they can appear at the end.

EXERCISE
Make a note of the trigger words in the chosen essay title. Compare your answer with ours.

The trigger word is quite simply '*What*'. It requires the writer to identify and explain the significant characteristics and strengths and weaknesses of the writer's own denomination. However, the trigger word 'What' appears twice and it is unclear whether the significant characteristics might themselves be regarded as strengths and weaknesses or whether these refer to something else. This is an issue that you as the writer have to address.

Finding resources and making notes

At an early stage in making a final selection of your essay title, it is important to ensure that you can resource it. Your resources for writing an essay include:
• knowledge and understanding that you already possess;
• notes from teaching sessions;
• relevant books and journal articles.

Knowledge and understanding that you already possess

EXERCISE
Begin by writing down your initial response to the title, based on your current knowledge. Spend from five to twenty minutes on this task (depending on your level of knowledge) and then check it with the possible answer below.

An initial response to 'What are the significant characteristics of your own denomination and what are its strengths and weaknesses?' might be:

Own denomination: Church of England

Significant characteristics
- a broad church containing Catholic and Reformed; high church and low church; conservative evangelical, traditional, liberal, and radical;
- organisation consisting of threefold ministry of bishops, priests and deacons; parishes, deanery, dioceses, provincial and synodical government;
- state church involving monarchy; House of Lords; education at church schools and colleges; a major Christian denomination; the parish church;
- liturgy including the word and the sacrament;
- resources drawing on scripture, tradition, reason.

Strengths and weaknesses
We found ourselves drawn back to our significant characteristics of the Church of England and how the first three of these at least might be regarded as both strengths and weaknesses. This finding may affect the way in which we would choose to write the essay.

These are initial thoughts and we may have omitted some significant characteristics. Some sections, for example, 'resources', relate closely to other areas like 'a broad church' and may at a later stage become subsumed within that section. Nevertheless, beginning in this way should engage your interest, build up your confidence that you know something about the subject and indicate some direction for further study.

The next stage is to look through any teaching notes or to move on to find relevant books or articles. Notice here that this essay title asks for significant characteristics and strengths and weaknesses of your own denomination. This might suggest that it would be helpful to consult both general works of reference about the church, in order to identify general and particular characteristics of your own and other denominations, and also specific texts about your own denomination.

In order to research the question you might use some of the resources described in chapter 2. For example, you might begin by using a dictionary of church history to help to set your denomination in its historical context, and a dictionary of liturgy and worship to examine the worshipping life of your church. If you are given a book list to help you to resource your essay, it is essential to refer to it and to use at least some of the books from the list.

Doing the research for an essay is, for some people, the most interesting part of the task. It should be about discovering new information and fresh ideas, or new perspectives on familiar subjects. Nevertheless, it is important to be disciplined about keeping focused on the task set by the essay title and you may find it helpful to look back to the methods of note-taking described in chapter 3.

It is important when making notes to use your own words to explain, summarise and evaluate the ideas or arguments from a text. If you are quoting, you must record quotations accurately and, whether using someone else's ideas or actual words, you must note the page number so that you can give an accurate reference. If you use phrases and sentences from your reading, without quotation marks and without referencing them, you will be guilty of plagiarism, which is a form of cheating.

Clarifying your argument and writing a plan

During and after each session of taking notes for your essay, it is helpful to review them and clarify your task. This may include reordering your notes so that they relate more closely to the question that is being asked.

Having begun the preparation for the essay by thinking about the title and writing down a preliminary response to the question, you are well on your way to having an essay plan. The question of how to revise your initial response now arises. Let us take as an example the revision of the preliminary response to the essay title, used in this chapter. The authors think that it would avoid repetition and contribute to a more coherent argument if each significant characteristic of the church that has been chosen for discussion is identified and analysed, and then evaluated as a potential strength or weakness. Moreover, the references to liturgy and resources made in the initial response appear on reflection to sit rather oddly with the other sections and might therefore be subsumed under the section on 'a broad church', as additional examples to be explored. The three main sections of the argument will also need to be broken down into separate paragraphs. The revised essay plan looks like this:

- A broad church containing Catholic and Reformed (for example, the liturgy includes the word and the sacrament); high church and low church; conservative evangelical, traditional, liberal, and radical (for example, resources used are scripture, tradition, reason); strengths and weaknesses.

- Organisation consists of threefold ministry of bishops, priests and deacons; parishes, deanery, dioceses, provincial and synodical government; strengths and weaknesses.
- State church involving monarchy; House of Lords; education at church schools and colleges; a major Christian denomination; the parish church; strengths and weaknesses.

The final stages of planning the essay are the introduction and the conclusion. In the introduction you will need to identify which denomination you are discussing, clarify your understanding of the question, for example, that the strengths and weaknesses of the church are part of its distinctive characteristics, and set the essay in its historical and ecumenical context. In the conclusion you will summarise your argument, perhaps drawing attention to the way in which the same characteristic can be both a strength and a weakness.

Writing and editing the essay

It is helpful to allow yourself a significant stretch of time, for example, three to four hours, to write a 1,500 word essay. Such a length of time allows you to become focused on your task, to concentrate on the argument of the essay and to keep the sequence of the argument in mind until the end of the essay.

It is important before you begin your essay to know the direction of your argument and your conclusion. The plan should have already demonstrated that this is the case. If you have planned your essay well and are in command of the subject you can really look forward to the actual writing.

The introduction may refer briefly to the context of the subject to be discussed, but it is important to ensure that you do not get side-tracked into, for example, an historical essay; you need to keep your title in mind. In the main body of the essay, try to find words and phrases to link the different paragraphs so that they move forward easily.

After completing the essay, it can be helpful to leave it for a time before reading it through, in order to gain some detachment from it and to encourage a critical reading of it. On your first read through you may choose to proof-read, that is, to correct any spelling errors. It can help to get this out of the way so that when you read for meaning you are not distracted. On the second reading you are concentrating on the meaning, that is, you ask yourself whether your argument is clear and convincing. Make any necessary alterations and correct any awkward expression before you submit the essay.

References and bibliography

In your essay you must provide the reference both for every quotation and also for every idea, argument or piece of evidence that you have taken from your resources. There are various ways of presenting references; these can be found at the end of this chapter. Every essay should also include a bibliography listing all the books and articles that you have used for the essay.

Analysis of examples of essay-writing

Three students, Cynthia, Terry and Rita, agreed to share with you some sections of their essays on 'significant characteristics' and the feedback that they have received.

EXERCISE

Examine one paragraph from the essay of each of our three students printed below. Comment on what you understand to be the strengths and weaknesses of their arguments and paragraph structures.

Cynthia

Here is Cynthia's section on 'strengths and weaknesses'.

> The tripartite theology of the Church of England should be one of the main strengths. Its authority is firmly rooted in the Bible which forms the basis of doctrine, teaching, creeds and liturgy. Article 6 of the 39 Articles states 'Holy Scripture containeth all things necessary to salvation so that whatsoever is not read therein, nor may be proved thereby, is not to be required of any man, but it should be delivered as an article of the Faith, or be thought requisite and necessary to salvation.'

> In the last century liberal theologians have attempted to challenge the authority, accuracy and truth of the Bible. While they have remained within the umbrella of the Church of England, they have

caused fragmentation, shaken faith and challenged the whole under-pinning of Anglicanism rooted in the Bible, by seeking to compromise some of the fundamental truths such as the virgin birth, Christ's death and resurrection and justification by faith alone.

The Church of England has been seen by many as trying to be 'all things to all people', and, in trying to encompass such a broad range of opinions and theology, has suffered a crisis of identity.

In 1837, Newman, Keble and Pusey in 'The Oxford Movement' brought more Anglo-Catholic doctrines into the Church of England.

Lately there has been a return to a more evangelical tradition in counteraction to the liberal theology of the past decades.

It is only when the history and traditions of the church, personal experience and reason by the guidance of the Holy Spirit, are rooted in the truths of the scriptures, that the balance of the tripartite theology is maintained and the church is strengthened.

Now compare your findings with ours. We consider that there is a clear statement of argument in the first sentence. Cynthia indicates that its tripartite theology is one of the strengths of the Church of England. She then cites one of the 39 articles as evidence of the importance of the scriptures as one of the three parts of that theology. She argues that this strength has been weakened by attacks made upon the fundamental doctrines of scripture by liberal theologians. However, she does not consider the arguments of the liberal theologians themselves and in this respect her argument is one-sided. Cynthia next suggests that the breadth of opinion and theology being 'all things to all people' is a weakness of the church. There seem to be two different but related characteristics of the Church of England here, one the tripartite theology and the other a broad church. It might have been helpful to differentiate between these and explain how and why each was a strength or weakness. Reference to the evangelical and Anglo-Catholic wings of the church provide further examples of a broad church, but they need to be fitted more securely into the argument. The last sentence re-introduces the two other elements of the tripartite theology (tradition and reason) but does not explore them as either strengths or weaknesses. In summary, Cynthia has gathered much relevant material and has begun to develop an argument, but her essay requires further separation, reordering and clarification of its different parts.

Terry

Here is Terry's section on 'strengths'.

> Whilst many obvious strengths are shown in the significant character-
> istics illustrated in the previous section, additionally the variety of
> Anglicans is widely accepted and acknowledged. This variety is
> increasing along with the increase taking place in the Anglican family
> and consequently Anglicans have enjoyed cultured variety through the
> nineteenth and twentieth centuries and their readiness to acknow-
> ledge this provides a constant source of enrichment. As a result much
> progress has been made by scholars in the understanding of the Bible
> recently and many issues have become clearer regarding the doctrine
> of the church and once divided Christians have come together. Most
> of what has been written on this topic and also the nearest to an
> Anglican perspective has been written by Roman Catholics. (This is
> derived from Sykes, 1996:21 and also Giles, 1995:2.)

Now compare your findings with ours. We will make three points
about Terry's paragraph. First, his initial sentence makes a good link
with the previous section but he does not capitalise on it by identifying
which of the characteristics were strengths. Second, the paragraph perhaps recognises two areas of strength: variety and openness to ecu-
menism. In both cases the exact meaning needs further clarification. To
what exactly does variety refer? Is it a reference to a broad church as in
Cynthia's paragraph, or does 'cultured variety' refer to the worldwide
Anglican Communion? Similarly it is not clear whether the recent work
in biblical studies refers to Anglicans of different backgrounds coming
together or Anglicans being open to dialogue with other churches.
Finally, Terry has quite rightly acknowledged his sources.

Rita

Here is Rita's section on 'weaknesses can become strengths'.

> Being a broad church is both a strength and a weakness. Its strength is
> its inclusive nature. The famous 'via media' philosophy has resulted in
> three 'parties' in the Anglican Church. They are the evangelicals who
> give priority to the Bible, the Catholics to the church (tradition) and
> the liberals to the mind (reason). Its weakness is that it tries to embrace
> irreconcilable differences. The first person to point out there were
> three divisions within the church was R Hooker in 1559: 'If Reason is
> seen as your top priority you are of liberal persuasion, if the Church is

seen as your top priority you are of Catholic persuasion and if the Bible is seen as your top priority you are of evangelical persuasion.'

'The Sea of Faith' (Don Cupitt) school sees the Bible, for the most part, as myth. They also have writings that see intercessory prayer as outdated and theologically impossible.

The 'Forward in Faith' group has severe problems with the ordination of women. They also make their own traditions in matters such as praying for the dead and in sacramental practices that Cranmer tried to outlaw.

The 'Reform' group threatens to split the church over doctrinal matters, especially homosexual issues, and it too worries about ordination of women.

The evangelicals have gained popularity as they have been seen to bring renewal to the church. They preach the gospel at all times and believe that conversion or being born again is a conversion of the individual. They join in the activities of the church, and believe in the Bible as a whole. Evangelicals could be classed as 'modern traditionalists' as they can be so outgoing to the point of disliking any other type of worship. The liberal theologians have ceased to believe in the personal active God, yet they continue to speak and write about God as though they do and the Anglo-Catholics are static and steeped in tradition, allowing no change to take place.

The strengths of having a bedrock of scripture is constantly challenging the secular society in which we live. Liberals keep the debate sharp and Catholics keep the church rooted in history. The weakness of the via media can be paralysis! Leadership is then weakened, as it constantly tries to accommodate three masters.

As a plumb line *The Book of Common Prayer* can attempt to keep the church from error, but its archaic language, and its sixteenth-century battles keep it from moving forward.

Now compare your findings with ours. We consider that Rita's first sentence captures well the complexity of the issue. She sets out admirably her argument that a broad church is both a strength and a weakness and the quotation from Hooker is excellent. The evidence for inclusivity and irreconcilability might have been more clearly set out. For example, the polarising of the three groups (liberal, traditional and evangelical) by referring to Cupitt, Forward in Faith and Reform is very effective, but its place in the argument requires further clarification. It seemed to be rather left in the air. The next two paragraphs beginning

'The Evangelicals ...' and 'The strengths of having a bedrock ...' continue to explore the three parties within the church but their place in the argument of strength or weakness might helpfully be further clarified. The final sentence about *The Book of Common Prayer* does not seem to fit with the rest of the argument. It is a good point but it does not belong here. Perhaps a closing summary indicating whether on balance she thought of a broad church as more of a strength or a weakness might have been more effective.

Bibliographies and referencing

There are several different ways of citing references in general use. You will see how these vary from one book to another as you read material written by different authors or prepared by different publishers. In the present series, *Exploring Faith: theology for life*, the editors have adopted a consistent style throughout the individual volumes. Our aim now is to explain how this style works. Unless the college or course you are following objects to this style we suggest that you adopt it for your own writing as well. If your college or course does object to this style they will provide you with their own alternative set of guidelines.

The system used in the *Exploring Faith: theology for life* series is a variant of what is generally known as the Harvard style. The Harvard style uses neither endnotes nor footnotes and is very straightforward to follow. The key to this style is this. Whenever you cite published material in your essay you include reference to the author's name, year of publication and the page from which you have drawn. This can be done in one of two ways.

- Evans (1999, p. 16) argues that the Gospel of Mark was written before the Gospel of Matthew.
- It is argued by some that the Gospel of Mark was written before the Gospel of Matthew (Evans, 1999, p. 16).

If you are referring to a publication written by many authors, you would cite it as follows:

- Evans, Lewis, Jones and Davies (1999, p. 16) argue that the Gospel of Mark was written before the Gospel of Matthew.
- It is argued by some that the Gospel of Mark was written before the Gospel of Matthew (Evans, Lewis, Jones and Davies, 1999, p. 16).

When a number of authors are involved, sometimes an abbreviation is used thus (Evans *et al*, 1999). We do not recommend this style.

Sometimes you may want to quote two publications written by the same author in the same year. Suppose Lewis wrote one book in 1998 called *Understanding the Baptist Church* and a second book in 1998 called *Understanding the Church of England* and you wanted to reference both books in the *same* essay, you would do so like this.

- Lewis (1998a) argues that the Baptist Church does not baptise infants while Lewis (1998b) argues that the Church of England does baptise infants.
- The Baptist Church does not baptise infants (Lewis, 1998a), but the Church of England does baptise infants (Lewis, 1998b).

Every author and date which appears in your essay must then appear in the reference section at the end, in alphabetical order. We recommend the following style. We have used italics for the titles of books and for the names of journals. The convention is to use underlining if italics is not available, for example when writing by hand. Give close attention to where we have used capital letters and where we have not used capital letters. Capital letters are used in the names of journals and in the titles of books, but not in the subtitles. The examples we give are not from real publications.

Books are referenced like this:

- Smith, R (1998), *The Four Colours: a study in method*, London, SPCK.
- Smith, R and Jones, J (1998), *The Four Colours: a study in method*, Birmingham, Alabama, Religious Education Press.

Note that the town comes before the name of the publisher. American towns are often followed by the state.

Journal articles are referenced like this:

- Smith, R (1998), The four colours: a study in method, *Journal of Theology and Art*, 16, 32–41.
- Smith, R and Jones, J (1998), The four colours: a study in method, *Theos: international studies in theology and art*, 16, 32–41.

Note that you need to give the volume number, followed by the pages on which the article begins and ends. There is no need to write out the words *volume* or *pages*. You will notice that journals are generally published with both a volume number and a part number. For example, volume 16 of *Journal of Theology and Art* might have been published in four parts in January, April, July and October. These would be known as 16 (1), 16 (2), 16 (3) and 16 (4). Although the volume was published in four parts, generally the page numbers follow on for the whole volume. In this case, 16 (1) would begin on page 1, but 16 (2) would begin on page 125 and 16 (3) on page 241. You do not need to cite part numbers *unless* each part begins on page 1.

Edited books are referenced like this:

- Jones, J (ed.) (1998), *Studies in Colour*, Oxford, Oxford University Press.
- Jones, J and Smith, S (eds) (1998), *More Studies in Colour*, New York, Oxford University Press.

Note that abbreviations are followed by a full stop when the last letter of the word is missing, but are not followed by a full stop when the last letter is in place: (ed.) but (eds). Note too that sometimes the town of publication may take you by surprise. Some Oxford University Press books may have been originally published in the USA and not the UK.

Chapters from edited books are referenced like this:

- Lewis, R (1998), Colour and texture in the nineteenth century, in J Jones and S Smith (eds), *More Studies in Colour*, pp. 42–67, New York, Oxford University Press.

Note that you need to provide the pages on which the chapter begins and ends.

Referencing for films, music, television programmes, newspaper articles etc. is very similar to that required for books and journals: include in your bibliography the same sort of details: who wrote/made it, what is the title of the piece, who published/broadcast it, and when.

Biblical referencing

When you quote or refer to verses of the Bible in your essay, you should give the book, the chapter and the verses, for example:

- Genesis 3:24
- 1 Corinthians 11:1–3

When you refer to more than one verse in the same chapter, separate with a comma, for example:

- Genesis 1:1–3, 6, 8

When you refer to two verses in succession you can use one of two styles:

- Genesis 1:1–2
- Genesis 1:1f

When you refer to a series of verses throughout a book or a passage whose end is difficult to identify you can use the following style:

- Toil is a prominent theme in Ecclesiastes 1:3ff.

When you refer to verses in different chapters or books, separate each citation with a semicolon, for example:

- Genesis 1:1–3, 6, 8; 4:5–6; 7:1; Exodus 4:3

Like other references, if you are quoting the source, the details of the reference should appear in brackets after the quote: 'In the beginning God created the heavens and the earth' (Genesis 1:1).

There are recognised abbreviations for all biblical books, which may be found at the front of most Bibles. We generally recommend that it is clearer to write out the name in full.

Authorship offers its own special problems. There are scholarly grounds for doubting, for example, that psalms ascribed to David are actually written *by* David. It might therefore cause confusion if you wrote, 'In Psalm 23 David says ...' There are ways around this. A preferable option would be to write, 'Psalm 23 states that ...' or 'In Psalm 23 it is apparent that ...' You might also legitimately refer to 'the psalmist' as author. Likewise with the Gospels you may refer to 'the Evangelist' or 'The Gospel writer'. Always avoid the generic 'the Bible says ...'

Further reading

Baxter, R (1995), *Studying Successfully*, Aldbrough, St John Publications (part 2, section 19).

Chambers, E and Northedge, A (1997), *The Arts Good Study Guide*, Milton Keynes, Open University Press (chapters 5 and 6).

Crème, P and Lea, M R (1997), *Writing at University*, Milton Keynes, Open University Press.

Fairbairn, G J and Winch, C (1991), *Reading, Writing and Reasoning: a guide for students*, Milton Keynes, SRHE and Open University Press (part 2).

Smith, P (1994), *How to Write an Assignment: improving your research and presentation skills*, Plymouth, How to Books.

Williams, K (1989), *Study Skills*, London, Macmillan (chapters 7 and 8).

5. DEALING WITH ASSESSMENT

Introduction

The aim of this chapter is to develop confidence in your ability to tackle assessment effectively as part of the learning process. We will examine three different areas of assessment:
- the criteria by which work is assessed;
- different forms of assessment:
    formal and informal,
    formative and summative,
    self-, peer and external assessment;
- methods of assessment other than essays:
    presentations,
    book reviews,
    projects,
    examinations.

Reflecting on experience

Think of two or three occasions in your life when your competence at something has been assessed. How did you feel and why?

On these occasions what did you find was the most helpful way of preparing for the assessment?

Do any of these 'lessons' usefully apply to the kinds of assessments you will face in your current course?

Criteria of assessment

If you know the criteria for assessment then you know what it is that the examiners expect of you. Criteria may differ slightly from institution to institution, but generally speaking the standards should be the same nationwide. Criteria will also vary slightly depending on the method of assessment, for example, an essay or a presentation, but there should be recognisable similarities between them. Let us consider some examples of criteria for assessment which are appropriate for an essay, a book review, an oral presentation or seminar, or a project. They are taken from a typical document on assessment:

- evidence of knowledge and understanding of the subject and/or texts;
- evidence of reading and use of other appropriate resources;
- quality of critical analysis and interpretation;
- quality of argument and structure (planning) of the assignment;
- evidence of critical reflection, personal or ministerial application;
- quality of communication skills and presentation.

The following describe the criteria given above more fully:

1. Evidence of knowledge and understanding of the subject and/or texts: to what extent does the assignment demonstrate breadth of knowledge, coverage of the topic, depth of understanding of issues, accuracy of information?
2. Evidence of reading and use of other appropriate resources: to what extent does the assignment show appropriate use of relevant, well-chosen and up-to-date literature and/or other source material, and an appropriate and accurate method of referencing?
3. Quality of critical analysis and interpretation: to what extent does the assignment demonstrate the ability to identify and analyse underlying issues, problems and questions and relate these to one another; to evaluate arguments and the evidence for them and examine their implications; to identify and to evaluate different perspectives?
4. Quality of arguments and structure (planning) of the assignment: to what extent does the assignment answer the question in a clear and direct way; form a coherent argument; develop in a logical and convincing way, relating the introduction to the conclusion?
5. Evidence of critical reflection, personal or ministerial application: to what extent does the assignment demonstrate critical reflection on evaluation of personal and/or ministerial practice?

6. Quality of communication skills and presentation: to what extent does the assignment reflect appropriate standards and academic conventions in relation to the mode of presentation, including clarity of expression, spelling, grammar and syntax, referencing and bibliography?

Levels of assessment

You will have noticed in the criteria above the recurring phrase 'to what extent'. It is the extent to which the assessment criteria are demonstrated that determines the mark awarded. Different levels of achievement of the different criteria are therefore described and related to bands of marks, which in turn may be translated into degree classifications.

We have already considered that essays requiring arguments, critical reasoning and evaluation cannot be a simple matter of right and wrong. Traditionally, it is very rare for students in humanities and theology to be awarded a mark of 75% or above. Indeed, in many institutions most students achieve a mark between 5–59%. This approach to marking is currently being challenged by some examiners who wish to use the full range of marks from 0 to 100. Others, however, are more cautious, because it would be a considerable change to begin awarding marks of 80% and above, possibly suggesting that standards had suddenly improved drastically. This debate will no doubt continue, but you may find it helpful to be aware of it and to ask about the policy of your own institution. Certainly, to be fair to all students, the issue needs to be addressed nationally, rather than by individual institutions promoting their own schemes.

There are three different conventions for expressing levels of assessment in general use. One convention uses percentage marks, a second convention grades from letters A to F, and a third convention speaks in terms of degree classifications. These three conventions can be placed side by side as follows:

• grade A, first class, 70% and over;
• grade B, upper second class, 60–69%;
• grade C, lower second class, 50–59%;
• grade D, third class, 45–49%;
• grade E, pass, 40–44%;
• grade F, fail, 39% and below.

For each of these grades clear levels are expressed in respect of each of the six criteria listed in the previous section.

1. Evidence of knowledge and understanding of the subject and/or texts

A. excellent coverage of the topic; accurate in detail offering sophisticated, even original insights; excellent use of examples to demonstrate understanding; clear understanding of complex ideas and issues

B. topic is covered in depth; detail is accurate throughout; independence of thought; good identification and understanding of complex ideas and issues

C. most relevant issues are covered with reasonable understanding; adequate knowledge is demonstrated; most central issues are identified

D. some relevant issues are covered; little evidence of ability to make connections between ideas and issues; there is partial understanding of the subject; little detail; reliance on anecdote

E. levels of knowledge and understanding are superficial and only just acceptable; detail is slight and not always relevant

F. there is some awareness of the demands of the assignment; there may be some misunderstanding of what was required; levels of knowledge and understanding fall below that which is acceptable

2. Evidence of reading and use of other appropriate resources

A. extensively researched in breadth and/or depth and accurately referenced

B. well researched and referenced

C. reasonable range of reading, sources not always explicit; not all referencing may be accurate

D. limited reading; over-reliance on a few sources; little evidence that sources have been used to enhance understanding; references may not be cited correctly

E. evidence of only superficial use of sources; references not properly integrated; referencing may be incomplete or inaccurate

F. claims made are usually unsubstantiated; sources have been misunderstood; referencing inaccurate

3. Quality of critical analysis and interpretation

A. imaginative, insightful, original, creative interpretations; impressive level of critical analysis and evaluation

B. perceptive, thoughtful interpretations; good level of critical analysis and evaluation; systematic analysis of source material

C. material from a variety of sources is drawn together in interesting ways; development of analysis may not be consistent, giving way to description

D. analysis is limited and is derived from very limited sources, giving way to description, paraphrase and opinion rather than critical comment; limited to a single perspective

E. little attempt to interpret or analyse material; work is mainly descriptive and presents unsubstantiated opinion

F. work is purely descriptive or polemical, lacking analysis and interpretation of sources

4. Quality of argument and structure (planning) of the assignment

A. a persuasive, authoritative coherent argument supported throughout by evidence, ability to show limitations of approaches; systematic and cogent structure

B. presence of a cogent argument, supported throughout by evidence; the work is well structured

C. demonstrates the ability to construct an argument and present supporting evidence; links between introduction and conclusion are made

D. argument or position not made clear; structure is loose

E. it is difficult to trace the argument; planning appears to be weak and/or confused

F. argument and supporting evidence absent or erroneous; little evidence of planning

5. Evidence of critical reflection, personal or ministerial application

A. evidence of sophisticated, critical reflection and evaluation of personal and/or professional/ministerial practice

B. evidence of critical reflection, understanding and evaluation of personal and/or professional/ministerial practice

C. some attempt is made to reflect critically and evaluate; reference is made to personal and/or professional/ministerial practice

D. there is limited critical reflection; there is insufficient discussion of personal and professional/ministerial practice

E. reflection lacks a critical dimension; there is mention, but no discussion of personal and professional/ministerial practice

F. any reflection is slight; there is little mention of personal and professional/ministerial practice

6. Quality of communication skills and presentation

A. written with flair and panache; fluent and confident; lucidly expressed and accurate in spelling and grammar
B. lucidly expressed and accurate in spelling and grammar
C. clearly written; there may be occasional errors in spelling and grammar
D. expression is uneven in quality, sometimes lacking clarity; style may be repetitive; inaccuracies in spelling and grammar
E. poor expression frequently obscures the meaning; errors in spelling and grammar mar the work
F. poor expression permeates the work; carelessly presented with many errors in spelling and grammar

Forms of assessment

Assessment is about measuring progress and achievement in learning. There are a number of different forms of assessment which can be combined and used for different purposes. We will begin by clarifying them. *Formal assessment* refers to the official assessments used by an institution to measure performance in relation to an award or qualification. *Informal assessment* refers to unofficial measurements of performance usually undertaken by the individual (self-assessment), peer (fellow student) or tutor.

Formative assessment measures progress in an, as yet uncompleted or uncorrected, assignment (or refers to completed work that does not contribute towards your final work). For example, if you ask a fellow student or tutor to read a draft of your next essay, you are undergoing informal, peer or tutor, formative assessment. This can be one of the most helpful forms of assessment in the whole learning process, as long as the feedback is accurate and specific, and you are able to address the issues which have been raised. *Summative assessment* refers to work which contributes towards your final mark or award. Although such marks provide a measurement of the standard of your work, the feedback which should be given with the result may be more helpful than the actual mark itself, in helping you to improve your next essay; thus, ideally, summative assessment is also formative. It is particularly important, if a mark has been unexpectedly low or disappointing, to receive feedback so that you know what went wrong and understand how to put it right.

Self-, peer and tutor assessment all make reference to the people who are measuring performance. Self-assessment is an important part of the learning process because it is about taking charge of your studies, and is always available. There are many obvious ways of engaging in informal, formative self-assessment, for example when you ask yourself whether you have understood all the parts of a lecture or discussion, or when you read through an essay before handing it in. Equally important, however, is the action plan that you make to address the issues arising from your self-assessment. Accurate self-assessment requires you to have accurate self-knowledge. For example, you may ask yourself whether you normally tend to underestimate or overestimate your level of performance. Perhaps you are a good judge of your own performance. Sometimes, self-assessment can be affected by moods or tiredness. This may be an argument for engaging in peer assessment.

Informal peer assessment operates whenever you ask a fellow student to read a piece of work for you. In seminars your peers will comment on your ideas or arguments. This can require some adjustment: to learn not to take assessment of your work as a personal attack on you. Of course, giving feedback also requires skill and sensitivity (see chapter 9). Sometimes peers become involved in formal assessment, but this is always alongside a tutor who will moderate the marks that are awarded. Clear guidelines should also be available for a task of this kind. Informal peer assessment, then, may confirm, disagree with, or add to your own assessment. It provides you with a more objective judgement and it can simply be more fun; learning to celebrate achievements and laugh at mistakes helps to keep them in proportion.

Tutors may take on two different roles in relation to formative and summative assessment. In the former, they may comment on your response in a discussion, pointing out its strengths and weaknesses, give feedback on drafts of essays and seminar papers, and so on. In the latter they are often examiners. They can still provide feedback but only after the assessment, without altering the mark gained. It is important for the learning process to take equal notice of feedback from both these types of assessment.

Other methods of assessment

Oral presentations

The criteria for assessment of a presentation are very similar to those for a written assignment, described earlier. There are, however, two main differences. First, a presentation is oral; the criteria for assessment will therefore measure your achievement of skills appropriate to this medium. For example, was your voice audible? Did you speak slowly enough for your audience to absorb your argument? Did you use appropriate visual aids such as overhead projector transparencies, video clips or computer software like 'Powerpoint'? Visual aids, however, are not compulsory; they serve only to enhance the quality that is already present in your arguments and evidence.

The second difference between an essay and an oral presentation is length. An essay is measured in words which can be counted simply by the word count on a computer; a presentation is measured in time. It is important to know how long your presentation should take and to stay within the parameters given. If your oral presentation is as short as five minutes then you must focus your argument sharply; do not try to cover everything. It is a good idea to practise beforehand, preferably timing it as you present it.

Book reviews

The aims of a book review are to give an overview of the main argument and the content, to provide an evaluation of the strengths and weaknesses of the argument and content, and to compare the book with others of a similar kind. It is important to be aware of your word limit in order to know how detailed and comprehensive your review should be. You should avoid a mere retelling of the contents of the book. You may find it helpful to read some book reviews in an academic journal before you begin your own work.

Projects

We are using the word 'project' to mean a combined theoretical and practical investigation or case-study into an area of applied theology and/or ministry, for example, 'An investigation into the spiritualities of members of the congregation in parish X' or 'Understandings of the Eucharist at church Y'. Projects such as these require you to combine a theoretical understanding of the subject that you are investigating, for example, spiritualities and the eucharist, with fieldwork such as participant observation, interviews and/or questionnaires which may record people's experience, knowledge, understanding and opinion. Projects may involve collaborative group work in which students assess one another's progress (see action learning sets in chapter 9). Not only are you required to use your skills of presenting arguments and evidence but you are also required to learn and use the necessary skills for conducting interviews and designing questionnaires in a professional and scholarly way. The advantage of such assessments is their practical relevance, but in no sense do they present an easy option because of the complexity of the integration of a wide range of knowledge and skills.

Examinations

Unseen examinations introduce at least three different elements into the assessment process: an externally imposed time constraint; a considerable element of dependence on memory, which is likely to disadvantage students of a more senior age and those with problems of short-term memory; an unusual, corporate yet individually focused experience, which many students find stressful. Nevertheless, examinations effectively rule out plagiarism and, through the process of revision, they may encourage a more holistic and comprehensive overview of a course of study. They also test the more usual skills of ability to construct an argument and to present supporting evidence. In order to prepare effectively for examinations, you should give yourself sufficient time to revise by planning a realistic revision schedule which allows for breaks and emergencies, and practise timed essays on a number of occasions so that you rehearse the skill of writing to time. It is as important to develop this skill as it is to revise topics and notes.

Further reading

Bourner, T and Race, P (1990), *How to Win as a Part-Time Student*, London, Kogan Page (chapters 9 and 10).
Race, P (1992), *500 Tips for Students*, Oxford, Blackwell.

6. KEY CRITICAL SKILLS

Introduction

In this chapter we are going to consider three of the key higher order skills which you will need to work on in the context of your study, namely analysis, synthesis and evaluation. These skills are part of the critical faculties we, as human beings, possess and use in everyday life. However, they are skills which all of us can work on and develop to sharpen our intellects and improve our powers of reasoning. They are part of the stock-in-trade of the serious student who will use them when reading the works of others or when writing. By way of background information, it may help you to know that such skills may be referred to as cognitive skills. Cognitive skills concern our abilities to know things intellectually. They are sometimes contrasted with affective skills which relate more to intuition and emotion.

Reflecting on experience

What do the three skills of analysis, synthesis and evaluation mean to you?

When in your everyday experiences do you apply the skill of analysis?

When in your everyday experiences do you apply the skill of synthesis?

When in your everyday experiences do you apply the skill of evaluation?

We will take each of these cognitive skills in turn and give you:
- a definition;
- examples of how we use the skill in everyday life;
- an example of the application of the skill in an academic context.

Through this approach you should be able to assess the level of your existing skills in analysis, synthesis and evaluation, and be able to work out an action plan for your further development in these areas. You will not be able to achieve mastery of these overnight. They will require constant attention throughout your academic study at whatever level. As you progress, so too will your cognitive skills. If you practise them consciously at the outset of your study programme, they should eventually become second nature to you. Even then, whether you recognise it or not, these skills should be at the heart of your approach to assessing the merits of someone else's writing or argument, as well as to assessing your own work.

Analysis

Definition

The word 'analysis' means to break something down into its constituent parts. In our context it concerns mainly the attempt to take an argument apart piece by piece so that we can expose the writer's main concerns. By doing this we are better able to understand the writer's argument or the position he or she takes on some issue. We can also then see how the writer makes connections between the various 'bits' or components which, together, make up the argument. This skill can also be used to help us plan our own essays, to help us identify the key ideas we wish to discuss, and to think about the order in which we wish to present them. It can also be used then to check our own work when completed to ensure that we have put an essay together in a structured way and in a way that enables us to make an argument as clear and as cogent (or compelling) as possible. The application of the skill of analysis is essential if we are to be able to unravel the complexities of an argument or to identify the key issues in a report.

How we use the skill in everyday life

You will find that you already use analysis a great deal in your everyday life and that you are quite competent at it. For the purposes of academic study, you simply need to focus it in a certain way and set about developing the skill with a greater degree of rigour than you may have used in the past. You are looking to build on the skill you already possess in order to increase your intellectual powers.

Here are some examples of how you already use the skill of analysis. You will be able to think of others that relate to home or work or even your social life. Perhaps you might make a list and note how some examples are more demanding than others in terms of their complexity and the knowledge you need in order to complete them:

- a shopping list (an analysis of the household needs for the coming week);
- following a recipe (identifying the ingredients and stages of operation in making a cake);
- decorating a room (an analysis of the various tasks to be performed, the order in which they need to be undertaken, the resources required in order to complete the task);
- planning a journey (identifying the various stages of a journey in order to get from A to B in the most efficient way);
- understanding a meeting where things took an unexpected turn (reflecting back on what was said in order to understand why things turned out the way they did).

It may be that up to this point you may not have particularly associated the skill of analysis with the examples we have given, but analysing is precisely what you have been doing when you have been engaged in these and similar tasks. In some of the examples we have given, the skill is being used as a means of planning something. You can transfer this skill to an academic context when you need to plan an essay or when you have to write a report. (In the next section we will show you how you can do this.)

There are also times when you will use the skill of analysis to check your understanding of some happening or event, as in the example above of the meeting. More frequently perhaps you will use it to check your understanding of something reported in a newspaper or magazine, or recounted in a television news bulletin or documentary. For example, in reading a newspaper account of a sporting fixture you may be interested to see how the game progressed, identifying, for example, when goals were scored or how long each set in a tennis match took. You may be interested in a political debate and read articles about it in order to identify the key issues at stake, or you may read the editorial of a newspaper to see which items of news the editor has identified for comment and what he or she has to say about each. Again this is a skill which you can transfer to the academic setting when, for example, you need to identify the key issues in a report or the main points in an article which you are required to read.

Breaking something down into its constituent parts enables you to see more clearly what the overall matter is about. It also provides you with a clearer understanding of what has to be done, either in the practical sense of stages in an operation or, more theoretically, by pointing up the issues that have to be taken account of if you are to gain a fuller grasp of the whole.

How we apply the skill in an academic context

We will use the following extract in order to apply the skills of first analysis and then, in the following sections, synthesis and evaluation. The extract comes from the book *Witness in a Gentile World: a study of Luke's Gospel* by Johns and Major (1991: 49–50).

> The way in which Luke presents the baptism of Jesus suggests that he was either less certain of the event's significance than was his predecessor Mark, or he felt it needed more cautious treatment than Mark had given it. For the earlier writer, the baptism is the point at which the story of Jesus begins. Jesus simply arrives on the scene without further comment, is baptised by John and, as he emerges from the water, the heavens open and there is a voice from heaven which says, 'Thou art my Son, my Beloved; on thee my favour rests' (Mark 1:11). These words are similar to those found in the Old Testament at Psalm 2:7. This psalm is about the coronation of one of Israel's kings. When a person became king, he was thought to be adopted by God and from then on would be treated as if he were God's son. As such he was God's representative on earth. In using these words, Mark is telling his readers that Jesus is God's new representative on earth. He is the Messiah whom the Jews have so long awaited. Luke has already made this point quite clear to his readers through the story of Jesus' birth so, in that sense, the baptism is not as essential to his gospel as it is to Mark's. Yet there is a need to mark the commencement of Jesus' ministry in some way and the baptism is an ideal way of doing this.
>
> Mark's account, as it stands, seems to present Luke with some problems, and he feels the need to modify it. Even during the early decades of Christianity's existence, ideas about Jesus were changing. Writing later than Mark, Luke is probably more consciously aware of the idea that Jesus in his earthly life had been sinless. So, Luke is faced with a

problem which Mark seems to have overlooked, namely, why was it that the sinless Jesus needed to be baptised when the purpose of baptism was to cleanse people from their wrong-doing and their old style of life and give them a fresh start? Matthew too seems to have recognised this problem, and he solves the matter by introducing a short dialogue between John and Jesus to give the reason for Jesus submitting to John's baptism. Luke does not do this. He chooses to play down the significance of the actual baptism by mentioning it almost in passing: 'During a general baptism of the people, when Jesus too had been baptised and was praying' (3:21). Note that John is not mentioned as the one who is doing the baptising, and Luke immediately puts the baptism in the context of Jesus at prayer (Jesus at prayer is a favourite theme of Luke's which he uses to mark significant moments in Jesus' life), so that what follows – the heaven opening and the Holy Spirit descending on him 'in bodily form like a dove', and the voice from heaven – is more to do with prayer than baptism. Perhaps Luke is emphasising that it is through prayer that one is filled with the Holy Spirit. (A similar point is made when Jesus is at prayer in Gethsemane, 22:39–46, and an angel brings him strength.)

Placing the baptism of Jesus within the context of a general baptism also enables Luke to show how Jesus identified himself with the ordinary people.

EXERCISE

What is the central concern of the authors in this extract (that is, what, overall, is this piece about)?

What are the main issues which the authors address (that is, what are the key areas discussed in this passage)?

In relation to this particular extract, the central concern is with Luke's treatment of the baptism of Jesus. The main issues are concerned with:
- the way in which Luke treats this incident differently from the treatment it receives in Mark and Matthew;
- possible reasons for this different treatment.

A fuller analysis of this extract would, however, require more detailed questions to be asked. These follow naturally from an identification of the main issues. So, in this case, an analysis of the content of the extract will show that, with regard to the two main issues, the authors make the following points.

With regard to the way in which Luke treats this incident differently from Mark and Matthew, the extract comments on:

- how Mark presents the incident;
- how Matthew presents the incident;
- how Luke presents the incident;
- how the three writers differ.

With regard to possible reasons for the different treatment, the extract comments on:

- how ideas about Jesus were changing in the early church;
- the purpose of baptism as understood by the early church;
- whether or not, given changing ideas about Jesus and a certain understanding of baptism, this helps us to think through possible reasons for Luke's different treatment of this incident.

This example has sought to show how the skill of analysis helps us to break down an argument or point of view into a number of constituent parts. Having completed an analysis, we can then look at whether or not an author has given fair treatment to each issue and how well the argument has been constructed.

We can also use this same skill if we are required to write, for example, an essay. Having given appropriate thought to the essay title, and completed the necessary reading, we can plan our essay using the skill of analysis to determine the main constituent elements of it and the order in which they should be developed so that the essay is coherent and cogent in its argument.

Using the theme from the extract on Luke's Gospel, the essay question might be: *Compare and contrast the presentation of the baptism of Jesus in Luke's Gospel with the same incident in Mark and Matthew, and give reasons for Luke's different treatment of the event.*

Your essay plan should be along the lines of the analysis of the extract identified above with the question being dealt with in two parts, namely:

- the way in which Luke treats this incident differently from Matthew and Mark, and
- the possible reasons for Luke's treatment of this incident.

The plan for the first part would need to include comment on the presentation of the incident in each of the three Gospels, drawing out ways in which they differ from one another. The plan for the second part would need to comment on possible changes within the early church during the writing of the three Gospels (especially concerning ideas about Jesus and the nature and purpose of baptism) which might help to explain Luke's different treatment of this event.

The same skill of analysis is used whether planning your own essay, and afterwards checking to see that it fits together well, or reading someone else's writing. If you pay attention to developing this cognitive skill, your academic work will be enhanced enormously.

Synthesis

Definition

The word 'synthesis' means to combine parts into a whole. You may be familiar with the word in a variety of contexts. It is often used to describe material that is made up from a number of ingredients. For example, garments are not always made of pure silk, cotton or wool but are described as synthetic, being made up of a range of natural and manufactured materials. In our context it is about the way in which we put together an argument or make a case in an essay or report. So, in a sense, we have already commented to some degree on the skill of synthesis, because we have talked about fitting an argument together so that it is coherent and cogent in the section on the skill of analysis.

Synthesis, then, leads on from analysis and can, in a way, be seen as part of that skill. However, its concerns range more widely and the skill of synthesis, though not complex to understand as a skill, can lead us into ever-increasing areas of complexity as we strive to be creative and innovative in our writing. For example, scholars working at the interface of disciplines may draw on ideas from more than one in order to make advances in an area of study. Thus, a theologian may need to venture into the realms of psychology and draw ideas from that discipline in order to shed light on, for example, some aspect of applied theology. In pulling together ideas and concepts from more than one discipline that can be shown to have a bearing on a discussion or an argument, the scholar is using the skill of synthesis. At this level of operation, the skill is a complex one. However, it is the same skill that may be used in a more straightforward way to plan the structure of a report or essay or, if you are reading an article or a book, to assess how skilful the author has been in putting the various component parts of the piece together as a whole. This, then, is an important skill in academic study and, as with analysis, can range from a fairly simple and straightforward use to much more complex levels of operation.

How we use the skill in everyday life

As a starting point for coming to terms with what is involved in synthesis, it may be worth thinking of the occasions in our everyday lives when we use the skill without naming it or considering it as such. This is important because it reminds us that it is a skill we already have competence in, and this competence will serve us well as we transfer the skill into an academic setting. If you can think of other examples of your use of the skill then make a note of them and think of what is involved in the process in terms of putting the bits together to create a whole. Here are some examples which may start you thinking about others which are more pertinent to you:

- organising a dinner party (inviting the guests, planning the various courses to complement one another, selecting an appropriate wine);
- planning the layout of a garden (deciding where the flower beds should be and what should go into them, where the vegetable plot should be located, and where and what shape areas of lawn should be);
- designing the décor and furnishings of a room (matching wallpaper, curtains, carpet and furnishings to give the room the desired effect);
- planning a garden party, fair or social event (co-ordinating the contributions of various people and organising the event as a whole);
- writing up notes taken during a meeting (incorporating the contributions of various individuals in setting out an agreed strategy).

The common theme in all of these examples is that of deciding how the various pieces of a task fit together to make an acceptable whole. This can be done either as a planning exercise or as a way of assessing to what extent the synthesising activity has been completed successfully. Part of the skill is also about identifying the parts themselves, and here you can see the close association between the skill of synthesis and the skill of analysis. In most cases there may be a fairly obvious number of parts to take into account (thus, with the example of planning a garden, flower beds, vegetable plots and lawns). There may also be less obvious potential parts to consider (for example, you could have a fish pond in the garden or a gazebo or a summer house). The skill of synthesis is, to some degree, about creativity and about making decisions as to which parts can justifiably be included in, for example, an argument. In academic work, this cannot be done randomly. You will need to be able to justify why you have included a particular 'part' into the whole.

How we apply the skill in an academic context

If we refer back to the extract from *Witness in a Gentile World* (Johns and Major, 1991) we can identify the 'parts' that have been used to make up this piece. In a way, we did that when we were applying the skill of analysis to it. Then we identified the following as the main ingredients:

- how Mark presents the incident;
- how Matthew presents the incident;
- how Luke presents the incident;
- how the three writers differ;
- how ideas about Jesus were changing in the early church;
- the purpose of baptism as understood by the early church;
- whether or not, given changing ideas about Jesus and a certain understanding of baptism, this helps us to think through possible reasons for Luke's different treatment of this incident.

Our present interest builds on from this and is about the way in which the authors have constructed this particular part of their book. The questions we need to ask now are about the creativity of the authors in arranging the material in the way they have, and also about the appropriateness of what they include. As soon as we engage in this, we are moving towards the skill of evaluation, about which there will be more in the next section. There is, then, some overlap between the skills of analysis, synthesis and evaluation as you are, no doubt, beginning to see. However, our concern at the moment is with the skill of synthesis and, in the context of our passage, we can see that the authors draw on their knowledge of a number of different areas of enquiry in order to deal with the issue of Luke's presentation of the baptism of Jesus. These may be listed as follows:

- Mark's Gospel;
- Matthew's Gospel;
- the early church and, in particular, changing ideas about Jesus, and the purpose of baptism within early Christian communities.

The writers draw on their knowledge of these sources of information in order to construct their argument or to explain their point of view. These sources inform their understanding of Luke's handling of the event of Jesus' baptism and help them to conclude possible reasons to explain why Luke presents his story in the way he does. To a certain extent, you must decide for yourself as to whether they have constructed their argument in a sufficiently convincing way. In so doing, you may stray beyond the realms of synthesis into style and presentation. This reminds us again that cognitive skills are not discrete entities and that we may be applying more than one simultaneously in assessing the value of a piece of writing. However, in order to get clear about the precise functions of each skill, it is worth spending time examining each as if they did stand alone.

We also need to ask, in relation to the extract on the baptism of Jesus, whether the sources the writers draw on are sufficient. To answer this, we may need to take into account the intended readership and level of scholarship aimed for. Thus, for a general introductory textbook on Luke's Gospel, we may conclude that the range of sources is sufficient. We may, however, decide that if this were a PhD thesis, they would not be. If we use the analogy of planning a garden, we might say that they have taken account of the flower beds, the vegetable plot and the lawns, but they have not given attention to the fish pond, the gazebo or the summer house. Without wishing to push the analogy that much further, you can see that limitations may be imposed upon you (for example, the size of the garden) or you may impose them upon yourself (for example, the cost factor).

When you come to write an essay or a report you too will be faced with making decisions about how to use the range of sources available to you, as well as taking account of some constraints, such as the pre-scribed length of an essay, or the level of study you have reached. As you progress, and your knowledge level of your discipline increases, so too will your creative potential for bringing together previously unrelated concepts and ideas that you see can be linked together in intelligible ways.

Many scholars choose to work in more than one related discipline because of the potential they see for linking them together. Dietrich Bonhoeffer, the German theologian, worked in the discipline of social philosophy (later to become sociology), when completing his first doc-torate, in order to illuminate more clearly the concept of church as com-munity. Some recent biblical scholarship has also drawn on the social sciences in order to shed new light on the Gospel writers and the Chris-tian communities for whom they were writing. Here, we can identify clearly the application of the skill of synthesis. Of course, you are not expected to operate at that level! However, the same process applies, and you will be able to transfer your present competence in synthesising to the academic setting, and develop that skill in an incremental way as you pursue your programme of study.

Evaluation

Definition

The word 'evaluation' means to make a judgement about something or to assess its worth or its value. In the academic context, evaluation is about assessing the strengths and weaknesses of, for example, an argument, an essay or a report. It may also be used to assess your own performance either written or oral, such as a presentation. In some cases you may be required to evaluate data of some kind (such as the results of a survey) or assess the value of primary source material (for example, an ancient document). The ability to evaluate is a highly prized skill in academic study, and it is certain that the better you are at it the higher your marks will be for your assessed work. It goes without saying that it is not an easy skill to master but the more you are conscious of the need to do it, and the more you work at it, the easier it will become.

How we use the skill in everyday life

All of us continually engage in the process of evaluation. We say that we like this dress or do not like that jacket. We select this colour rather than that when decorating a room, and so on. The problem with this form of evaluation, however, is that it is not always entirely rational. Choices of this sort may be motivated by a range of emotions and experiences, or may simply be a matter of personal opinion or preference. There is also the danger of irrational bias creeping in or, worse still, some form of narrow-mindedness, prejudice or even bigotry. Perhaps it would be safer not to use the word evaluation at all in such contexts, especially in cases where people are not conscious of why they are making certain choices rather than others. However, the choices we make about virtually anything are evaluations, even if they are not thought through very well or prove to be very profound. Clearly, in the context of academic study, the level of your skill of evaluation will be judged by how well you are able to think through issues clearly and thoroughly. This will involve you in weighing up both sides of an argument before arriving at any decision. Giving reasons why you have ultimately sided with one view rather than another is crucial.

If we identify some examples where you already engage in the process of evaluation you may be able to consider how accomplished you are at this skill in everyday life, and identify some further examples to reflect upon:

- planning a holiday (considering the reasons why you prefer one resort to another, and taking account of issues like travel arrangements and cost);

- applying for a job (weighing up the benefits of a new opportunity over against the security of the known);
- reporting an event to a third party (perhaps summarising a sporting event you had witnessed or a meeting you had attended);
- decision-making of any kind at home or work (giving careful consideration to the options open to you);
- buying a car (considering size, shape, colour, and so on in relation to your needs).

In each of the above examples you could make an ill-thought-through or hasty decision on what to do or say, or you could think a matter through carefully, weighing up the pros and cons before arriving at a decision. Any one of us could undoubtedly give dozens of examples of when we have made poor evaluations as well as when we have thought things through with care before deciding. Of course, you may be fortunate in everyday life and find that things do turn out well, even if you do not subject them to careful thought. This is not the case, however, in academic study, where you are required to demonstrate a degree of rigour in your thought processes. Each time you make a judgement about something, you should be in a position to offer reasons in support of that judgement.

How we apply the skill in an academic context

In the extract from *Witness in a Gentile World* (Johns and Major, 1991) which we have been using, the authors give reasons why they think Luke deals with the baptism of Jesus in a way that is different from the treatment this event receives at the hands of Mark and Matthew. Our job as students is to evaluate their claims and to make a judgement as to whether the case they argue for is a reasonable one. We have already completed an analysis of the extract and, in so doing, have identified the issues we need to consider in our evaluation. These are the questions identified:

- Are the authors right in saying that Luke treats the baptism of Jesus differently from Mark and Matthew?
- What other evidence might there be that ideas about Jesus were changing in the early church?
- Are the claims that are made by the authors concerning the early church's understanding of the purpose of baptism supported by the evidence?

Having identified the issues for consideration, what methods are we going to use in order to be able to undertake some form of evaluation? In the case of the accounts of Jesus' baptism in Mark and Matthew, we can go directly to the source and read the Gospel narratives for ourselves. This is made especially easy for us if we can gain access to a synopsis, where the texts of the first three Gospels are set out in parallel columns. Here we can see immediately if Luke's account is indeed different from the other two Evangelists and in what way. We also need access to commentaries, the purpose of which is to help the reader to understand more clearly the meaning of the text. By examining what other scholars have to say about this particular passage from Luke's Gospel, we will be able to judge whether the authors of our extract are saying something different about this passage or whether there is a degree of consensus about it. We may need to consult the commentaries and other textbooks on Luke's Gospel, as well as books on early church history, in order to check out the claim made by our authors that ideas about Jesus did change and develop during the first centuries of Christianity. This will help us to assess whether it is reasonable to conclude that the process is evident in the Gospels themselves.

By the same token, we will need to check out the early church's understanding of the purpose of baptism, perhaps by starting with the entry on baptism in a theological dictionary, and checking further in the textbooks on early church history. By undertaking this sort of thoroughgoing enquiry we should be well placed to make an overall judgement about the quality of the argument and the reasonableness or otherwise of our authors' claim that Luke presented his account of Jesus' baptism in the way he did in order to overcome some of the difficulties he had detected with Mark's account.

We hope to have shown that when you read an article or the chapter of a book, there will be a number of things to evaluate. Earlier we noted the close association that evaluation has with the other two cognitive skills which are the concern of this chapter. Thus, we can make a judgement about the way in which an author has constructed a piece of writing, and here we blur the distinction between evaluation and synthesis. We may choose to comment on the author's style and presentation, making a judgement about that. It may be that we choose to comment on the way in which the author has used the sources available, noting whether we think they have been used fairly or whether they have been manipulated to suit the author's own ends. We will need to assess the worth of an argument both in its parts and as a whole.

This is not something that you are expected to do alone. Scholars spend much time writing about one another's work and so you can usually pick up clues and ideas from reading around your subject. Even to examine the views of two scholars on a common subject, noting that one concludes X and another concludes Y, is a form of evaluation. If you are then able to go on to say, on balance, that you side with the X view rather than the Y, and are able to give clear reasons for the position you have taken up, then you have increased the depth of your evaluation.

You can also use this skill as a form of self-assessment. Careful reading of an essay of which you have completed the first draft may enable you to improve it if you subject it to critical evaluation. You should be able to spot whether you are making your argument clear enough, and to strengthen with evaluative comment any areas that you feel may be too descriptive.

Finally, be reminded again that you are not expected to gain mastery of these cognitive skills overnight. They will, however, improve gradually as you get further into your studies but only if you are conscious of what they are and aware of the need to apply them constantly to everything you do.

Further reading

Bourner, T and Race, P (1990), *How to Win as a Part-Time Student*, London, Kogan Page (chapter 4).

Evans, C F (1990), *St Luke*, London, SCM and Trinity Press International.

Fairbairn, G J and Winch, C (1991), *Reading, Writing and Reasoning: a guide for students*, Milton Keynes, SRHE and Open University Press (part 3).

Johns, E and Major, D (1991), *Witness in a Gentile World: a study of Luke's Gospel*, Cambridge, Lutterworth Press (chapter 6).

7. MORE CRITICAL SKILLS

Introduction

The purpose of this chapter is to introduce you to more of the key skills the student needs to develop, and also to increase your awareness of the wide range of learning opportunities which life affords us. You will have noticed that the word 'critical' is used in the chapter heading. When we use this word in the context of academic study we mean 'to make an informed judgement about something'. We do not mean, as we so often do when we use the word in everyday language, 'to point out someone's faults or failings in a destructive way'. Words, of course, are notoriously difficult to define. Sometimes the same word can have several different meanings and sometimes different words can mean the same. You will need your wits about you in this chapter, and you may wish to question some of the definitions we use.

Reflecting on experience

Consider your own ability to make critical judgements. Think of recent critical judgements you have made. How much do you trust your own critical judgements?

Has your work on the earlier chapters in this book sharpened your ability to make critical judgements? If so, in what ways is this demonstrated?

Knowledge and understanding

When we say that we 'know' something we are usually referring to 'facts', that is, to information that is available to everyone. Facts, we may say, are about objective knowledge. Thus, if anyone challenges a fact, we ought to be in a position to demonstrate its truth or reality. If, for example, we lift the bonnet of a car, we can see parts of the engine. Even if we do not know the names of the parts or their functions, that information is widely available; experts know and they could tell us.

Knowledge is of vital importance in any form of study. It provides the raw material or data with which the student works. For example, it would be important for anyone studying twentieth-century Christianity to *know* that the Second Vatican Council is the name given to a series of meetings called by Pope John XXIII, held within the Roman Catholic Church during the late 50s and early 60s of that century. It is possible for anyone interested in Vatican II to gain further detailed knowledge about it: many books have been written on the subject. Without that knowledge it would not be possible for anyone to *understand* the changes that have come about in the Roman Catholic Church since the Council.

There are, of course, far more things to know in any area of study than any one of us actually knows. Nevertheless, in principle, that knowledge is available for us to learn about if we have a mind to do so. Gathering knowledge can be great fun and can lead to a great sense of achievement. Knowledge, it has been said, is power. Almost certainly as we grow in knowledge we feel empowered.

You will undoubtedly amass an amazing amount of knowledge during your course of study but knowledge alone, it may be said, is not enough. Along with knowledge we need understanding. It is all well and good to be able to identify the parts of the car engine that we see when we lift the bonnet, and to know what function each performs, but to be truly knowledgeable about engines we need to understand how all of the bits work together in order to make the engine run. Similarly, to understand about Vatican II we need not only to have facts about it but to know about wider issues such as the situation the Roman Catholic Church found itself in at the time of the Council, and the period which led up to it and how the church changed as a result of the Council. That is, to understand something we need to be able to hold all the bits of knowledge together in a reasoned way and see them as a whole.

Understanding, then, leads on from knowledge and helps us to make sense of a number of facts, or of the pieces of knowledge, relevant to an area of study or enquiry. Because most of us have great difficulty in remembering all of the facts concerning a matter, understanding is an important cognitive level to achieve as, in some sense, it enables us to see the 'whole' without having to remember the detail. Having grasped the whole picture, an important breakthrough has been achieved and we are secure in the knowledge that we can always, at a later date, look up any facts we once knew but may have forgotten.

To summarise, we may say that you cannot have understanding without knowledge but, conversely, knowledge without understanding is of limited value. In academic study both are needed and it is usual for tutors, when marking student assignments, to work to criteria which include *knowledge* (for example, to what extent accurate knowledge of Vatican II is demonstrated) and *understanding* (for example, what evidence is there to indicate understanding of the place of Vatican II in the history of the Roman Catholic Church during the twentieth century). It is also likely that other assessment criteria will include *evaluation* (see chapter 6), which is often regarded as the next stage of the cognitive process. Having gained knowledge of the facts, or pieces of information, they can be connected together so that understanding of the full picture emerges. This picture can then, in turn, be evaluated in terms of its significance or importance. Thus, we may know about the parts of the engine, as well as the way in which the parts function together, but we may wish to go on to ask how useful is the engine. We may, for example, wish to make some assessment of its level of performance or its sophistication in relation to other engines we know of, and so on. Similarly, with the Second Vatican Council, we may wish to evaluate its contribution to the life of the Roman Catholic Church today, or assess the impact it has had in the context of the ecumenical life of the Christian church.

The three cognitive skills of knowing, understanding and evaluating are mutually dependent and students are usually required to demonstrate ability in all three in most assessment tasks. You cannot, for example, understand something if you do not have accurate information (knowledge) about it. In turn, you cannot evaluate something of which you have little or no understanding.

To take a different example: *knowledge* of the Christian doctrine of providence is provided by a definition of the concept; our *understanding* of it is tested by our ability to explore its implications and connections with other doctrines; whereas *evaluation* is the process of assessing its comprehensibility, truth and value using criteria such as meaningfulness, evidence, coherence, moral worth and personal impact.

As you engage further with your academic studies be conscious of what you are doing and try to achieve a balance in terms of your intellectual engagement with the material that comes before you. So, be aware of when you are 'information gathering', of when you are making some sense of all of the bits together, and when you are making a judgement about the impact or usefulness (or whatever) of the subject of your study. Remember that most assignments will require you to demonstrate your ability in all three parts of the process. This means that when you are writing an essay you need to make sure that there is an appropriate balance between its more descriptive and its more critical parts. You also need to be aware that it is likely that in most assignments a higher proportion of marks will be allocated to the use of the more critical skills (such as evaluating) than for the more descriptive demonstration of knowledge.

To make this clearer we will refer again to the extract from *Witness in a Gentile World* (Johns and Major, 1991) which we used in chapter 6. Here you will find examples of both descriptive and more critical comment woven together to produce a piece of continuous prose. It can be analysed as follows:

> The way in which Luke presents the baptism of Jesus suggests that he was either less certain of the event's significance than was his predecessor Mark, or he felt it needed more cautious treatment than Mark had given it.

A judgement is being made here, so this would count as demonstration of the skill of *evaluation*. Clearly there could be other ways of interpreting what Luke is doing in his presentation of Jesus' baptism. If you were writing an essay on this topic and using this book as a resource you would be advised to check what other commentators have to say before deciding how accurate you think our authors are in their assessment.

> For the earlier writer, the baptism is the point at which the story of Jesus begins. Jesus simply arrives on the scene without further comment, is baptised by John and, as he emerges from the water, the heavens open and there is a voice from heaven which says, 'Thou art my Son, my Beloved; on thee my favour rests' (Mark 1:11).

This amounts to entirely descriptive comment. Anyone who has a mind to can read the relevant passage and check out the 'facts' (what the text says) for themselves. The repetition of *knowledge* in this context is justified because it serves the purpose of setting the scene for the reader. It goes without saying that the description needs to be accurate but, in the minds of most markers, descriptive writing will not gain vast amounts of credit because it is expected that information gathering will be done accurately, and that quotes will be clearly identified as such and properly referenced. So, when you are writing an essay, include in it only as much description as is necessary to make your discussion intelligible. Do not overdo the description. Of much greater importance in the minds of markers is your *understanding* and *evaluation* of the material. They will know that your success in using these critical skills results from your mastery of a certain amount of relevant *knowledge*.

> These words are similar to those found in the Old Testament at Psalm 2:7. This psalm is about the coronation of one of Israel's kings. When a person became king, he was thought to be adopted by God and from then on would be treated as if he were God's son. As such he was God's representative on earth.

This is mainly about *understanding*. The writers are able to relate the passage under consideration to wider knowledge concerning kingship in the Old Testament. In so doing they demonstrate their ability to connect bits of knowledge from various sources to create an understanding of the whole picture.

EXERCISE
Read the rest of the extract from *Witness in a Gentile World* (Johns and Major, 1991:49–50) and see if you can analyse it in terms of knowledge (description), understanding and evaluation.

Experiential learning

In whatever form of study we are engaged upon, the critical skills we have discussed in this chapter so far and in chapter 6 are crucial to our success. What we aim to do in the rest of this chapter is to increase your awareness of the range of learning contexts available to us. Reading a book or listening to a lecture provide us with formal learning contexts, and these are vitally important to every student, but we should not restrict our understanding of learning opportunities to schools, colleges, universities, libraries and rooms we call studies. That would be far too limiting. Most of us probably learn most of what we know in other contexts, including our work and our involvement in clubs, societies and churches, as well as the home. In such contexts we are busy 'doing' and we do not always recognise that we are learning. When we do not have the *intention* of learning through what we are doing we learn incidentally, haphazardly and partially.

There is, however, an educational philosophy which recognises the potential of the less formal learning opportunities which all of us experience daily, and argues that, if we have the intention of learning through these experiences and can identify them and structure them, a method or strategy for learning can be devised. The name given to this form of learning which starts from the experience of the individual is *experiential learning*.

Experiential learning is not haphazard and incidental but planned and systematic, though it is always open to redefining learning needs in the light of changing circumstances, and is always open to the possibility that unplanned-for learning opportunities may arise. It identifies in advance what the learning potential of an experience (for example, a strategic development related to your job or a project you are undertaking for the church) is, or is likely to be, and determines methods for accessing the learning. Having identified the likely learning outcomes, the student then engages with the experience (that is, gets on with the job or the project) and, having completed the task, reflects on the process and assesses to what extent the learning planned for in advance has been achieved, and what unplanned learning has occurred.

As can be imagined, such learning draws on a wider range of learning resources than are usually encountered in other forms of learning. This points to the richness of experiential learning and to its inter-disciplinary nature. It does not in any sense have the intention of setting aside books and theories or anything else associated with our conventional understanding of learning. On the contrary, it sees what we are accustomed to calling 'academic' learning as a crucial part of the experiential learning process. However, what drives experiential learning is the perceived learning needs of the student. Instead of the student being told by an 'expert' what is on the syllabus, the student is to a much greater degree responsible for designing the syllabus for himself or herself. The identification of the need for theory will arise out of the action (that is, the experience) itself.

For example, someone who is asked to assist with the Sunday School by taking a class of ten-year-olds may identify in advance some of the learning he needs to access in order to be able to do his job effectively. This may include gaining knowledge and understanding of the syllabus and, beyond that, further biblical and theological study in order to underpin its content. There may also be an awareness of the need for some understanding of teaching methods which may, in turn, lead to the need for accessing a considerable amount of education theory. However, the precise learning needs may not be known or fully realised at this stage. These will be refined and sharpened in the light of experience.

The experiential learning cycle

This is the name sometimes given to a process which involves the student in first taking some sort of action (for example, our new Sunday School teacher who delivers his first lesson). Having acted, the student then reviews or reflects upon what happened in the action. For example, he may start by asking himself a number of questions, such as: What went well? What went not so well? What really did not work at all? If he is undertaking this reflection as a serious learning opportunity, he will note down the learning he achieved.

For the purpose of recording his thoughts in a systematic way, he may keep a Learning Journal, with headings for action, analysis, evaluation and reflection. It may work something like this.

- **Action** describes what he did, for example, *told story of 'Good Samaritan' in context of lesson on 'caring for others'*.
- **Analysis** identifies what went well and what went not so well, for example, *my telling of the story engaged the children but they were distracted when I tried to have a discussion with them about it.*
- **Evaluation** assesses why something went well or badly, for example, *I told the story very energetically and I think it was my enthusiasm which held their attention. Discussion did not go so well because the children were over-familiar with the story and I had not got sufficient theological understanding of the story to introduce new ideas to them.*
- **Reflection** identifies what has been learned from the experience and, perhaps just as importantly, identifies what further learning is needed in order to do the job more effectively, for example, *I need to be more selective with illustrative material and introduce something new that will move the children on in their thinking. I need to find out about other biblical stories which would provide suitable illustrative material for the topic, ensuring that I understand their theological significance.*

In dealing with his post-action enquiry in this way our Sunday School teacher is engaging in the skill of *critical reflection*, that is, he is looking back (reflecting) on the experience and making a judgement (which is what the word 'critical' means) or judgements about it. Critical reflection is a prized skill and perhaps the single most important key skill in any form of experiential learning. It is one which, like the other cognitive skills we have already spoken of, requires effort and practice if it is to be developed to a high order. Yet, again, it is one of those skills which all of us are acquainted with in some shape or form from our daily lives, albeit perhaps in less sophisticated ways. All of us have undertaken tasks which we have subsequently reflected on in terms of how well we did (for example, building a fish pond in the garden) and how much easier it would have been if we had had certain knowledge available to us (for example, knowledge of different types and qualities of lining material, and how to install an electric pump for the fountain), and thought about how we might have done things differently or how we would *act* next time. Perhaps we have not previously reflected on experiences of this sort in any depth, but hopefully you can see the potential for adopting a much more critical stance towards them.

If we return to the experiential learning cycle and to our Sunday School teacher, the next stage is for him to undertake the learning he identified in his Learning Journal. Here he recorded what he needs to go on to learn to do his job more effectively. This is the point at which more traditional forms of academic learning may need to be accessed. He may have realised that he really did not know enough about the particular passage of the Bible that formed the core of the previous week's lesson, or concluded that he really needed a wider background knowledge of the Gospels to deal with the sort of questions the children were asking. Libraries and textbooks now need to be consulted in order for the necessary knowledge and understanding to be gained.

Having equipped himself with this greater knowledge, the Sunday School teacher is then able to move into the next phase of the cycle which is to *plan* for the next lesson. His thinking about this will now be informed by the academic study he has undertaken and so his preparation will be more thorough and, informed by the previous week's experience, he can shape the material more to meet the particular needs of the children in his group. He then completes the cycle by *taking action* (that is, delivering the next lesson) and, at the same time, starts the next cycle by reviewing his performance and making notes about it in his Learning Journal. Through this method, learning that is needed for the precise requirements of the job in hand is achieved. In this way, the Sunday School teacher will build up a considerable amount of academic learning in the area of biblical studies to underpin the syllabus he is teaching. But learning of the experiential sort is almost inevitably multi-disciplinary. Learning about the content of the syllabus is not enough to make our Sunday School teacher a success. He will also need to pay attention to the teaching methods he uses and subject them to the same experiential learning cycle. He will also come to see that not all of the children in his group learn in the same way (for example, he may note in his Learning Journal that some prefer to *do* things rather than to sit and listen to him talking, and that to talk to any of the children for more than ten minutes is pointless because they have lost concentration after that time, and so on). These observations and reflections on experience may lead him to consult books on educational theory where he may learn about such things as individual learning preferences and styles of learning (see chapter 8). Again, when planning for the next lesson, his new learning will inform his thinking.

The experiential learning cycle can go on indefinitely, though perhaps we should think of it as a spiral rather than a cycle. Although the process is cyclical, the learning hopefully reaches higher levels with each operation of the cycle. Whether we think of it as a cycle or a spiral it is clear that the reflective practitioner always has more to learn from experience. For example, you can imagine that our Sunday School teacher will go on learning about the Bible, Christian theology, child cognitive development (the entry in the Learning Journal may read, 'They did not understand the ideas I presented them with this morning'), and so on.

The experiential learning cycle also offers a great deal of potential for the Sunday School teacher to learn more about himself so that, as well as learning about the Bible and Christian doctrine, teaching methods and children's learning, he is also engaging in critical reflection upon his own life. He may wish to note (again, using the Learning Journal) how this greater involvement in the work of the church is affecting him as a Christian, and what influence it is having in terms of his relationships with others (for example, wife, children, work colleagues, fellow Christians). He may be able to chart something of his own spiritual development and see this as part of the learning process. If he examines his experiences in the light of his own faith, especially in relation to the teachings of the Bible and the church, he is engaging in *theological reflection*.

EXERCISE

Before reading the next section, pause briefly to consider a learning experience you have recently undergone. (It can be something quite simple, like using a mobile phone.) Ask yourself what you did, how you learnt and what you learnt. Looking back, see if you can apply the experiential learning cycle to the process of learning.

Complete a Learning Journal entry to get the feel for how useful this method of recording your reflections might be.

Theological reflection

Theological reflection follows exactly the same method as any other form of critical reflection. The principal difference is that the 'theory' that is used when reflecting on action, and on thinking about and planning for the next action, is of a *theological* nature. Thus, key resources are the Bible (especially the teaching of Jesus), the historical and contemporary teaching of the church (especially on what God is like and how the Holy Spirit works in the world), Christian ethics and values, and so on. In the example of our Sunday School teacher, it is less easy to tease out precisely what the theological elements of his reflections are because of the nature of his learning agenda. However, if we take an example of someone facing an experience or undertaking a project in their everyday work, we can perhaps identify more clearly what is involved in theological reflection.

Let us suppose that an office manager has been instructed to design and put in place a new method of working which involves setting aside the existing hierarchy and getting her colleagues to operate more as a team. The making public of her initial proposals indicates that there will be much resentment from those who had previously been regarded as section leaders, and the idea of staff development training in team working was generally being treated with contempt. In subjecting this, and any other situation, to theological reflection a range of approaches is possible, and the situation itself will usually suggest the most appropriate starting points. For example, after initially reflecting on what has happened and how she can move things forward, it may be that the manager starts by asking herself what light, if any, the Bible can throw on to this situation. In particular, perhaps, she may consider whether there are any incidents in the Bible which come to mind that have some bearing on the experience. Is there some saying of Jesus which seems relevant? Alternatively, perhaps the Old Testament prophets will offer some insight into the issue. Maybe the only thing that starts the ball rolling for the manager is Jesus' saying, 'Do to others as you would have them do to you' (Matthew 7:12).

It may be, then, that this theological reflection causes our manager to imagine how she would feel in this situation. She uses the skill of *empathy* in order to increase her awareness of how her colleagues are feeling. Perhaps she concludes that their reaction has come about because they were not properly consulted or asked to share in the planning of changed working practices. They have been told what is going to happen to them and they have been left feeling powerless and alienated by a situation that is not of their own making. The manager is aware that Jesus was one who stood up for the rights of the oppressed and the down-trodden and, whilst the situations Jesus found himself in were very different, nevertheless it could be argued that the principle is the same. Similarly, the Old Testament prophets, especially Amos, have much to say about those with power who mistreat the powerless, and so on. There is no exact parallel situation to be found and we should not expect to find one, but there is enough about how we should treat one another for us to be able to establish some principles that may be applied to the situation, and for our manager to decide upon a new course of action which takes much more account of the feelings of the people involved. However, as well as some feeling disempowered, others of our manager's junior colleagues may feel empowered by a situation of team-working where the opinions and contributions of all members of the team will count. What, if anything, can the Bible offer here? Is Paul's teaching about the body being one but having many parts (1 Corinthians 12) of any help? As with so many situations we encounter in life, this one is complex and there may be no easy solution.

Further theological reflection on this experience may be done in relation to *church tradition* (or the history of the church's teaching). What may occur to our manager, when reflecting on this, is part of the very recent history of the church and an on-going movement within it, namely that of liberation theology. Reflections on the situations which gave rise to liberation theology, and the solutions of some theologians working within that movement, might lead our manager to consider that not only must she take account of the feelings of those involved, but that she may need to challenge the decision of her line managers to change working practices on the grounds of justice and fairness. There are, on the other hand, those within the manager's office who will be empowered by the proposed changes, and so she needs to reflect on their interests in the light of liberation theology and consider how their rights can be maintained.

It will be apparent to you by now that what is being suggested by way of theological reflection is dependent to a large extent on a knowledge of the Bible and of church tradition which many people may not have. There are, however, ways of accessing that knowledge through talking with others in the Christian community. Indeed, sharing a matter of concern with others (keeping in mind that some issues to do with work may be confidential and may have to be dealt with in general terms) is, in itself, another way of engaging in theological reflection.

The whole array of academic theological resources is also there to be accessed. This will be essential in terms of gaining a deeper understanding of the biblical or church teaching that is being used to help us consider our actions and experiences against. The same degree of critical thinking is as important in theological reflection as it is in any other form of critically reflective scholarly activity.

Other factors which our manager will need to include in her reflections include the context in which this matter has arisen, for example, the prevailing culture of the organisation and whether this is part of a general shift in ways of operating (this, in itself, may be reflected upon theologically). It may be that team-working as opposed to rigid hierarchical structures is more appropriate. She will also have her own past experience to reflect upon and what she may consider to be her God-given reason (that is, the power to discern God's will through her own intellectual capacities). Issues of ethics and values have already surfaced (for example, what is the right way for an employer to behave towards her employees) and will never be far away. They underpin Jesus' actions and teachings as well as those of the Old Testament prophets and liberation theologians, and any decision the manager takes will reflect her beliefs and values. In the light of her theological reflections, the manager may plan for her next action by taking into account a far wider range of issues than she had originally considered.

EXERCISE

By way of consolidating your understanding of the process of theological reflection, pause for a moment to see if you can apply the method to a recent or current matter which concerns you. Ask yourself, for example, if there is some aspect of the teaching of Jesus which you can reflect on in the light of your concern, or if what Christian teaching has to say about God throws any light on the subject. Identify what academic resources you might use in order to deepen your understanding of some area of Christian theology which you believe may be relevant to your concern, and consider what other resources are available to you.

Further reading

Carr, W (1997), *Handbook of Pastoral Studies*, London, SPCK (chapter 6).
Green, L (1990), *Let's Do Theology*, London, Mowbray.
Kolb, D A (1984), *Experiential Learning*, New Jersey, Prentice Hall.

8. LEARNING PREFERENCES

Introduction

In chapter 1 we encouraged you to think about your own learning achievements to date. Undertaking a review of this sort should not only have boosted your confidence but also have made you aware that learning is a continuous process, some of which is achieved in formal learning contexts and some in less formal ones. In this chapter we aim to raise your awareness not so much about *what* you have learned but about *how* you have learned it. We aim to get you to think about the methods of teaching and learning which suit you best and also to think about other methods to which you may not have given much consideration or have set to one side.

Unless we are good all-round learners, and few of us probably are, each of us, as you will see, has his or her own preferred learning style or styles. It is our learning style which inclines us towards one teaching and learning method rather than another. Through introducing you to the idea of learning styles, we hope that you will be better equipped to judge how *you* learn best, that is, to identify your own learning style. However, having identified the methods through which, and situations in which, you learn most effectively, we hope that you will see that your overall performance as a learner could be vastly improved if you moved beyond the 'comfort zone' of your preferred learning style and ventured more into other territories of learning.

Reflecting on experience
Consider the following six different learning contexts in light of your previous experience. Decide which one (or ones) suits you best. ▶▶

Context A Learning seems most accessible when I sit and listen to a teacher or lecturer who obviously knows his or her subject well and can impart knowledge in an engaging way (for example, lecture room).

Context B I learn best when left to my own devices with a number of books on the topic I am interested in. Through reading and making notes on my reading, I can engage with the topic and learn effectively (for example, study, library workstation).

Context C Learning seems to come most easily to me when I sit down and talk with others who share my interests and concerns (for example, seminar, action learning set, informal discussion group).

Context D The situations in which I find I learn most easily are those where there is a practical element involved. I like to get my sleeves rolled up and be actively engaged in something where I can find things out for myself: learning by trial and error (for example, workshop, field-work, work-based learning).

Context E If someone shows me how to do something, I find that I can learn to do it myself quite quickly and easily (for example, demonstration, workshop, work-based learning).

Context F When I have finished a task I like to look back on it and consider how well I did it and where I can improve next time. I find that I learn most effectively that way (for example, study, library workstation).

There may be other learning contexts which you could add to the list drawn from your own experience. These may be memorable to you because they yielded positive learning. It is clearly not the case that one learning context is better than another; it is simply that, from the individual learner's perspective, one context may be more congenial than another. Identifying your own preferred learning situation(s) is obviously important. It is also important, however, that you consider how you might improve your performance as a learner by moving into contexts that are outside your 'comfort zone'. This should increase your potential for learning, or at least make you aware of a wider range of learning opportunities than you may have previously considered.

Theories about learning preferences

We will introduce you to three theories about learning preferences so that you have some models to reflect on in terms of your own self-understanding and so that you can see the potential of developing yourself as a more all-round learner.

The Herrmann whole brain model

The learning situations which we find most congenial are, of course, not to do with the situations themselves at all but are about the way in which we use our brains. Some interesting work has been done on this by an American psychologist called Ned Herrmann. Herrmann argues that each of us has the potential to operate as thinkers and learners in each of four dominant areas and, if it helps, we can think of our brains as being subdivided into these four quadrants, each of which can be characterised in the following way:

Quadrant A

'A' is the logical and rational quadrant which is comfortable with factual matters, analysing issues, quantifying and critiquing and generally being at home with mathematics. Those who are dominant thinkers in this quadrant are likely to be authoritarian in attitude and may view life as a series of problems or challenges which can be met and dealt with through the application of one's critical faculties. Learning may be seen as mastering a body of knowledge which has been provided for them to work on. 'A' quadrant thinkers may be effective as independent learners.

Quadrant B

'B' is the ordered, organised and controlled quadrant, which seeks to establish systems and ways of handling data and detail so that life is regulated and planned. Dominant thinkers in this quadrant like to be in charge and may be good organisers and administrators who see life as a matter of bringing order out of chaos and who enjoy planning and developing systems to ensure that life runs smoothly. Learning may be regarded as a matter of identifying bits of knowledge which only make sense when they have some order imposed upon them so that they can be controlled and used effectively.

In some ways, 'A' and 'B' have much in common. Together they may be spoken of as left brain qualities, and those who possess them may appear to be so involved in facts and figures and plans and their implementation that they lack an awareness of people and the emotional side of life. In this respect, they differ from those who are sometimes referred to as possessing right brain qualities.

Quadrant C

'C' is characterised by a greater concern for people and things associated with the more emotional and spiritual side of human existence such as art and music. People who are 'C' oriented enjoy being and working with others, talking and expressing ideas, and they generally find the interactive and interpersonal aspect of being human fulfilling. Learning may be most effective when ideas are shared and matters are talked through. Contact with teachers and other students may be highly valued.

Quadrant D

'D' is the ideas and imagination quadrant where matters are viewed holistically and resolutions to problems and challenges are conceived of and visualised in the mind's eye. Thinkers in this quadrant tend to be creative and inventive, and enjoy coming up with fresh ideas and new solutions. They may prefer learning in unstructured ways and in contexts where they are free to explore ideas and come up with their own thoughts.

Those who possess the so-called right brain qualities of the 'C' and 'D' quadrant may appear to be less well organised and more concerned with people and with ideas than they are with thinking things through in an ordered way and with getting the job done.

It might be interesting if you pause for a moment in your reading to reflect on where you see yourself in relation to this model. You might also recognise other people you know: perhaps a colleague at work or a relative or friend. Because a person is strong in one area does not, of course, mean that they do not also operate in other areas. They do but, in some respects, their qualities elsewhere may be overshadowed by their dominant characteristics.

Clearly Herrmann uses a metaphor when he thinks of the brain in this way, and we have to recognise that the qualities associated with each quadrant are no more than caricatures. Even so, it may be helpful as a way of understanding ourselves a little better and for making sense of why some learning contexts seem to be more congenial to us than others. Herrmann devised a detailed questionnaire designed to enable a profile of the participant's relative strengths in each quadrant to be drawn up. Used as a diagnostic instrument, individuals can then see where they need to concentrate attention in order to develop themselves in areas where they may be less comfortable or where they are under-performing. If you are interested in reading about Herrmann's ideas, you can consult Herrmann (1993), *The Creative Brain*.

Even without the test, however, it may not be too difficult for each of us to recognise ourselves and others as being dominant in one or other of the quadrants, and as possessing the characteristics described. You may note, for example, that either in yourself or in someone you know, the qualities of two of the quadrants are combined. Thus, a good manager may be someone who combines both 'B' and 'C' qualities, whereas a sound business person may be someone who combines 'A' and 'D' characteristics, and so on. The important thing for you as a learner is to 'know yourself' and to be able to recognise your own strengths and weaknesses as a thinker and learner. If you can do that then you can more easily devise strategies to aid yourself in your learning. You will know better than anyone else those areas of thinking where you are less comfortable. For example, you may be a well-organised person who enjoys planning and implementing strategies but you may feel that you lack ideas and vision. On the other hand, you may be someone who has lots of ideas and imagination but rarely sees anything through to its conclusion because you lack organisational skills. In either case, greater self-awareness is the first step in finding a way forward. The next is to consider how some of the approaches to learning spoken of in this book may help you to move beyond your present 'comfort zone' into new learning contexts. In particular, you might wish to consider how collaborative learning (the subject of chapter 9) might be of benefit to you.

The Kolb experiential learning cycle

Another way of reflecting on our own potential as learners is to think back to chapter 7 where we discussed the experiential learning cycle. In David Kolb's version the stages are understood in terms of action, reflection, theorising and planning. Kolb identified these as essential parts of the process of experiential learning but also claimed that each of us is likely to have a preference for *one* of these stages. In other words, each stage can be seen to represent a preferred learning style and so some of us will prefer to be *active learners* with an emphasis on 'doing', while others of us, having had a 'concrete experience', will be good at *reflecting* on it in some depth, analysing it in terms of what went well and what went not so well. There are those of us who are more comfortable with libraries and books, where we can read about and study ideas and theories, and there are those of us who enjoy planning and determining how to act in the future. Again, you may be able to recognise immediately your own learning preference or preferences (you may be comfortable in more than one area), and you may be pleased to discover that it is quite natural that you have one! However, this should not lead you to complacency because, clearly, a more ideal situation is to be a good all-round learner. Indeed, to complete the experiential learning cycle effectively, each of us has to demonstrate some facility at each stage and, of course, we are all quite capable of doing so. The whole point of identifying our preferred learning style is to help us to identify more accurately where we need to improve our performance, thus engaging in purposeful self-development.

Kolb developed what he called the Learning Style Inventory to help individuals to identify their strengths as learners, but also to pinpoint for them areas for development. If you are interested in testing yourself on Kolb's Learning Style Inventory you can consult Kolb, Rubin and Osland (1991), *Organisational Behaviour: an experiential approach.*

The Honey and Mumford Learning Styles Questionnaire

In a similar way, Peter Honey and Alan Mumford developed the Learning Styles Questionnaire. This is again designed to assist individuals in identifying their own learning style or styles, with a view to aiding their own self-understanding and potential for self-development. In identifying four learning styles and designating them 'activist', 'reflector', 'theorist' and 'pragmatist', Honey and Mumford are not significantly different from Kolb and the learning styles he derived from the experiential learning cycle.

According to Honey and Mumford, *activists* are keen to get on with the job and enjoy new challenges, while *reflectors* are more cautious and stand back from the experience in order to consider it from all angles. *Theorists* tend to be logical thinkers, who are concerned to undertake research in order to arrive at rational conclusions, while *pragmatists* are keen to plan for and try out new ideas to see if they improve practice. Again, if you are interested in taking the Honey and Mumford Learning

Styles Questionnaire, you can consult Honey and Mumford (1986), *The Manual of Learning Styles*, for the full test and administer it to yourself, checking your answers against the scoring sheet provided.

It is, of course, not necessary to take either the Kolb Inventory or the Honey and Mumford Questionnaire in order to improve your all-round learning potential, though the results do provide feedback which may jolt the subscriber into a new level of self-awareness, or at least confirm his or her own self-understanding.

Learning styles and assessment

As a result of reading this chapter, our aim is that you will have increased your knowledge about yourself as a learner and that you will find this useful in a number of ways, including in the context of assessment. You may discover, as you get into your studies, that you find certain assessment methods more congenial than others. For example, an open-ended project assessed by means of a portfolio may better suit the person who is strong on ideas and imagination, while the more traditional essay and examination may appeal to those who are more comfortable when given a clearly defined body of knowledge to analyse and evaluate. Others, who are more people-oriented, may find presentations and other forms of oral assessment more congenial, while creative types may relish non-traditional forms of assessment such as the production of works of art, videos and other forms of display.

If there is the opportunity on any of the courses you take to negotiate the assessment method, and there may be in some enlightened institutions, you may consider it worth your while to play to your strength. On the other hand, with your increased self-knowledge as a learner, you should be better able to consider ways in which you might prepare yourself more thoroughly for a specific assessment method with which you are less comfortable, for example, by finding ways of remembering information if it is an unseen examination, and undertaking mock timed-essay writing; allowing yourself time to have the first draft of an essay looked at by a tutor; giving a presentation to a group of friends and getting them to provide you with some honest feedback, and so on.

Self-understanding

The purpose in including this brief excursion into learning theory is to get you to think about yourself as a learner and to provide you with some tools for analysing your own strengths and weaknesses in this regard. Our view is that the better we understand ourselves, the more equipped we are to become effective learners. Glance back at the list of typical learning contexts provided earlier in the chapter and consider how you might increase your learning potential by testing out contexts where previously you have felt less comfortable or disinclined to try. Progress may be slow at first because these contexts may not be the natural settings in which you learn best but, by gently moving into them, you are beginning to extend your repertoire of learning opportunities and are using your brain more effectively. Remember that each of us possesses all of the qualities indicated by the three learning style models we have presented you with, but does so in different measure. Where we feel less comfortable in a learning context it is probably because we are not naturally inclined to the method of learning that the context provides. Because we feel that we are not playing to our strength in such a situation, we may under-use the capacity we actually do possess, leaving that particular area underdeveloped. The more we persevere in learning contexts we find less congenial, the more likely we are to develop our capacity as learners in those areas and, thus, overall improve our all-round learning potential.

We would also encourage you to consider how this brief introduction to learning theory may help you to assess your actual patterns of behaviour in the world beyond your studies, for example, with reference to your performance at work or your contribution to the life of the church. It may be that your new-found awareness may help you not only to assess your present level of activity but also your potential contribution as a member of the communities you serve. Those actively involved in various forms of ministry in the church will be well aware that the full range of attributes identified by learning theorists are required for effective operation. You need to be 'good with people' but also strong on organisation. Creativity and imagination are called for but so, at times, is a more disciplined and analytical approach to a matter. Perhaps this is not so different from life in general where we are frequently called upon to be good 'all-rounders'. We are of the view that, when individuals assess their own strengths and weaknesses, their increased awareness of themselves has an immediate impact. Having models to reflect on, such as those we have considered in this chapter, gives you a frame of reference for reflection and perhaps some understanding of who you are as you are. This knowledge may be the first stage in bringing about change and development in your own life if that is what you want. Such development may lead you into new work activities or new areas of ministry, enabling you to further the contribution you already make to the communities of which you are part.

Further reading

Herrmann, N (1993), *The Creative Brain*, Lake Lure, North Carolina, Brain Books.

Honey, P and Mumford, M (1986), *The Manual of Learning Styles* (fifth edition), Maidenhead, Peter Honey.

Kolb, D A, Rubin, I M and Osland, J S (1991), *Organisational Behaviour: an experiential approach*, London, Prentice Hall.

9. COLLABORATIVE LEARNING

Introduction

You will have noticed that throughout this book we have placed the emphasis on *learning* rather than teaching. Given that it is a book intended for adult learners that seems appropriate and sensible enough. However, it is worth drawing out the point because it is so easy to become dependent on teachers and lecturers and, in so doing, sacrifice your own independence as a learner. This is not a desirable situation for a number of fairly obvious reasons. First, no one can learn for you; it is something that only you can do for yourself. Second, dependency is not a healthy condition anyway, and it is inclined to breed resentment if things do not work out as well as hoped for (for example, blaming the lecturer when you do not know something, or feeling that a better teacher would have taught you a lot more). Third, it implies a rather passive approach to learning which, although appropriate in some settings, may prove overall to be rather limiting as a learning strategy.

We are saying this not in any way to undermine the value of teaching or to deny its central importance for most of us as learners, for all of us need good teaching and good teachers, but to make the point that, as learners, we have an active role to play. We need to see learning as a collaborative activity, and all of us should be prepared to accept responsibility for our own learning from the outset. As implied in chapter 2, teachers are perhaps better viewed as facilitators or as learning resources, among a number of learning resources available to us, rather than being seen as the key to knowledge. Taking control of your own learning puts *you* in the driving seat and is a crucial step in becoming an independent learner. Adult learners, in particular, need to be independent learners, not only because it is the only condition that is worthy of their status as adults, but also because they often have so many other commitments to weigh in the balance (work, family, friends) that only they can be in control of their own learning.

> ### Reflecting on experience
> Reflect on your own life situation and your own attitude to learning in the light of what we have said, and ask yourself how prepared you are, at the present time, to become the manager of your own learning.
>
> Then reflect on your own experience of higher education to date, even if it is quite limited, and ask to what extent you have been welcomed into, and see yourself as part of, a learning community.

The learning community

It has become customary in recent years for some people to speak of educational settings as learning communities. This is an acknowledgement that, whether lecturer or student (paid employee or paying customer), all of us are learners. Universities and university teachers are, among other things, committed to research and, by definition, research is a learning activity. Thus, when you join a university or college you are joining a community of learners. Admittedly some may be further down the learning road than others, but even the most able of professors is a learner who treads a very narrow learning pathway when seen in the light of the unbelievable breadth of knowledge and information that exists in the world. The notion of the learning community also implies that those joining it must bear responsibility not only for their own learning but also for other people's learning. This means that you not only join a course in order to learn and to be taught, but also in order to aid others' learning and to be a teacher in some sense yourself. Your teaching may not be of the formal variety but you will be able to contribute to the learning of others in various ways. Given the old adage that the best way to learn is to teach, you may decide that getting together with other learners in informal sessions to share information is to the mutual advantage of all concerned.

The skill of attentive listening

It seems reasonable to argue that there can be no such thing as passive learning and that all learning is, to some degree, collaborative. All learning, if it is to be learning, requires some form of activity on the part of the learner. Listening is an activity, and being a good listener is quite a skill in itself. Being an attentive and critical listener may not come naturally to all of us, and it may be a skill that we need to develop. It is all too easy to be preoccupied with our own thoughts when someone is talking to us. The danger then is that, at best, we only hear what they say from our own point of view. Being an attentive listener requires us to employ, to some extent, the listening skills of the counsellor. In this context, and to help us get clearer on what is involved in attentive and critical listening, we will comment on the three core conditions, crucial in interpersonal relationships, identified by Carl Rogers (1983). These are *genuineness* (that is, having a genuine concern to enable the partner in dialogue to grow), *unconditional positive regard* (that is, being prepared to challenge the assumptions and views of the other person but in a spirit which values and supports them) and *empathic understanding* (that is, putting yourself into the place of the other person in an attempt to see things from their point of view).

EXERCISE
Reflect on your own position in dialogue with others to check out the extent to which *you* operate with these underlying principles. You will probably not find it too difficult to assess the position of others with whom you have dealings!

Active and critical listening is crucial when attending lectures and seminars if we are to maximise their learning potential. Simply attending a lecture is not necessarily a learning experience unless we *actively* choose to make it one. It is easy enough to go through the motions and to come away with little idea of what the lecture has been about. Even if the lecturer is having a bad day and is presenting material in a less than coherent manner, we still have some responsibility, as self-managed learners, to ensure that we gain something from the experience. If the content of the lecture is not making sense, then you should not be afraid to interrupt and ask for clarification. If the lecturer is making what you consider to be controversial claims, offer some response which indicates that there may be other points of view to consider. Unless it is a very formal lecture to a large group, say 50 or more, it is usually appropriate to offer an intervention if it is in the interests of your learning. Believe it or not, most teachers actually welcome 'interruptions' because it indicates that what they are saying has aroused interest, and because they know that often the most fruitful part of a lecture period is when there is a dialogue and engagement with the learners. Questioning and discussion indicate that the learning process is occurring and, therefore, is affirmation for teachers that they are being successful in their work. Clearly interventions need to be necessary and managed sensitively. Constant interruptions, especially on relatively minor points, can be annoying to other members of the group, especially if they are not having the same difficulties as you in grasping an issue. As suggested in chapter 2, therefore, it may be more convenient for everyone if you make a note of a particular difficulty you seem to be having so that you can discuss it with the lecturer at a later time, rather than engage in persistent interruptions during the course of the session.

A collaborative model of education

To sum up what has been said so far in this chapter, we could point to the contrast which the liberationist thinker and educationist, Paulo Freire (1972), makes between the transmissive or 'banking' model of education and the 'dialogical' model. The former is passive, with the teacher regarding the learner as a container to be filled. In this view it is the teacher who possesses the knowledge that the learner needs. Thus, knowledge is seen as a gift given by the wise to the ignorant. To take the 'banking' analogy, the learner's account is empty until the teacher starts making 'deposits' of knowledge. The implication is that the more lessons you attend (that is, the more 'deposits' that are made), the richer (that is, more knowledgeable) you will become. By contrast, Freire sees the dialogical model of education as a much more collaborative and interactive process. The notion of dialogue in itself presupposes an equality between teacher and learner, and implies that knowledge (or meaning or truth) is arrived at by a process of 'talking through' the issue, with each partner in dialogue contributing something to the process. In Freire's view the 'banking' model of education keeps the learner oppressed (that is, under the control of the teacher and less inclined to develop the skills of critical thinking), whereas the dialogical model is liberating, making the learner responsible for his or her own learning and for developing the skills of critical thinking which characterise the educated person.

EXERCISE

If part of your learning experience involves attending lectures, reflect on essentially which model of education the lecturer is working with. If it is the transmissive model, you might wish to consider in what ways you can compensate for the 'power' loss you are suffering as a responsible self-managed learner.

When called upon to 'teach', consider your own understanding of the learning process in relation to the model you adopt. Teaching inevitably involves imparting knowledge, but that in itself is not necessarily a denial of the dialogical model. Would you agree?

Co-operative working

Much benefit can be gained from viewing learning as a collaborative rather than a lone activity. In chapter 8 we pointed to the potential of working with someone who has a different learning style from your own. For example, if you are a good organiser but find yourself short on ideas, then talk with someone who is good on ideas. When you talk something through with someone else it often has the effect of sparking off ideas and thoughts of your own. So, use other people as resources for your own learning and allow them to do the same with you. This is not an infringement of Rogers' three core conditions if you each share the same agenda and give each other the same learning opportunities. We have had a tendency in the past in the UK to make education competitive. Tests and examinations sometimes reinforce this idea and make education a rather lonely and isolated occupation. In this competitive environment, education becomes a rather private and individual affair where the sharing of information and ideas is discouraged either explicitly or implicitly by virtue of the system. While tests and exams may have some virtues, they may also work against the sort of climate for learning that many educators would wish to cultivate. This alternative climate sees education occurring in contexts where co-operation, collaboration and partnership flourish. It therefore encourages team working, and joint projects where ideas can be shared and developed and where joint presentations and reports may be used for assessment purposes. However, we should not overlook the point that what we have just described as a learning process may appeal strongly to Herrmann's 'C' quadrant person, whereas the approach which culminates in the examination room may be more appealing to someone from quadrant 'A' (see chapter 8). This reminds us that a variety of teaching styles and assessment methods will be desirable if the needs of a wide range of learners are to be met.

Team working as an aid to learning

We are aware that for some of our readers weekly (or more frequent) meetings with other learners is a feature of their experience, while others may be working at a 'distance' and in relative isolation from learners who are following the same or a similar programme of study. In either case, opportunities to share ideas with others outside the context of formal meetings may be few and far between. We feel, therefore, that some consideration needs to be given to the potential benefits of learning in the context of a peer group or team. Such groups may occur informally or may be deliberately planned for as a strategy to aid learning. We will suggest that members do not necessarily have to share an interest in the same subject content; it is commitment to the process or method as a learning strategy that binds them together.

Social psychologists' distinctions between what constitutes a team and what constitutes a group need not detain us, but it may be worth noting that their definitions of both typically include a reference to *achievement of shared goals in a spirit of co-operation and inter-dependence*. Working within a group or team where these features exist can be an empowering experience both for the individual and the group. For some people this 'community' approach to learning may be quite difficult to adjust to, so used are we to living as 'individuals'. We may have to learn to live in community in order to participate effectively in a group or a team. This we may regard as a valuable learning experience in itself, and an important part of developing self-understanding.

EXERCISE

Before reading the next section, consider your own feelings about group learning informed, perhaps, by your own self-assessment of your preferred learning style (see chapter 8). If the idea does not seem immediately appealing, you should not be concerned. It simply means that, at present, it is outside your 'comfort zone'. However, try to read what follows with an open mind and, perhaps, in the future be prepared to take a risk by moving outside your comfort zone of preferred learning experiences. Calculated risk-taking, remember, is a very important part of self-development.

Action learning sets

A particular way of working as a team, where the shared goal is for each member to achieve completion of, and success in, some task, is to form an action learning set. The principal intention of an action learning set is the empowerment of individuals to take responsibility for action on issues which are important to them in their lives. On this point, it is the *process* of the action learning set that is relevant because it creates an atmosphere where openness and trust within the group are of paramount importance, and where members commit themselves to supporting one another in challenging but constructive ways. An action learning set may ideally consist of four to six people, each with a specific task they need to complete. In our context that may be the completion of a particular course of study or part of a course; it may be the task of becoming a more effective learner; or it may be a time management issue (such as, given a hectic lifestyle, trying to find the time and energy to study). Whatever the task, the aim of the action learning set is to provide a platform and supportive context for the individual to explain and to think through the challenge he or she is facing. It does not assist directly, for that would be to undermine other people's responsibilities, and the aim of the action learning set, as already stated, is to empower individuals to meet their own goals.

Typically the set will decide how much time can be allocated for the consideration of the issue each individual wishes to bring to the group. (This will depend on how much time the group as a whole can set aside, but it would usually be no more than half an hour for each person.) In turn, and sticking strictly to time, each individual will be able to outline, without interruption, the nature of the challenge (using perhaps no more than ten minutes to do so). During that time the other group members give the presenter their undivided attention. The quality of attention each set member gives to the presenter is of prime importance in action learning sets. The amount of support and encouragement given by set members through their attentive listening (not, at this stage of presentation, by their verbal interventions) is vital to the amount the presenter is prepared to disclose. It also indicates that the set member is not a passive listener and, among other things, is attempting to understand matters from the presenter's point of view.

Following the description of the situation, members will question the speaker on the issues, on action already taken, and on plans for further action. The aim is to prompt the presenter to consider the challenge from all angles and to get him or her to think through all the alternative courses of action available. It is not the job of the group to tell the presenter what to do or to give advice as such. The group does bear the responsibility of ensuring that no one questioner attempts to hijack the discussion for their own ends or dominates the conversation. It is also crucial that high-quality interpersonal relationships operate throughout and, therefore, that the three core conditions identified by Carl Rogers apply. The quality of usage of these three core conditions will determine the quality of the experience for the presenter. The questions which the set members ask will reflect the extent to which they have empathised with the presenter. These questions will be designed to support and to challenge in supportive ways the presenter's assumptions and provisional conclusions so that he or she may be better able to make an informed decision about future action. To be prepared to give this degree of time and energy unconditionally to another person is a considerable commitment, but it is one that is demanded by membership of an action learning set.

As can be seen, the process is a simple one, but the abilities required to be an effective member of an action learning set are considerable. They are not, however, any more demanding than the qualities all of us ought to strive for in terms of our relationships one with another. Where an action learning set works well, the skills of attentive listening and empathic understanding will create possibilities for greater disclosure on the part of the presenter and, through feedback from set members, may lead to increased awareness on the part of the presenter about himself or herself (opening up the 'blind spots'), and greater knowledge of the presenter on the part of set members (breaking down the facade). Such openness can only occur in an atmosphere of trust and confidentiality.

Benefits of joining an action learning set

Clearly it can be seen that bonds are likely to develop between set members and there is learning to be had about one another as well as about oneself. What, however, about action in relation to the task that has to be completed? The last five minutes of a half-hour time slot allocated to each set member should be used by the presenter to summarise his or her thinking in relation to the task, and commit himself or herself to a course of action. This proposed course of action is agreed by the set members to be realistic and achievable within the space of time available before the next meeting of the set (frequency of meetings will be decided by the group depending on circumstances but may typically be weekly, fortnightly or monthly). At the next meeting, each member knows that the same process will be repeated. This means that when it comes to presenting, the set will want to know whether the action to which the presenter had committed himself or herself at the previous meeting had been undertaken and with what results. They will listen attentively and without interruption while the presenter outlines what was done and with what consequences before asking questions and perhaps challenging the interpretation of events given by the presenter.

We hope that the potential for your own learning of working as a member of an action learning set is clear. The individual members may have different personal goals, that is, not all of them are necessarily doing the same course as you or perhaps not even on a formal course of study at all. They will, however, have some task or another which they need to complete and this may be related to work or to their personal lives. The shared goal is the successful completion of the various tasks. You can bring to such a group the issues which are of concern to you in the completion of your present course or study module. For example, you may be having difficulty in understanding the lectures, you may be faced with preparing a seminar paper or giving a presentation and may not be entirely sure how to go about it, even after advice from the tutor. You may have to undertake research for an essay and be having difficulty in obtaining resource materials or even getting started on thinking about the topic. Through the process of talking through your difficulties in an open way and in a context where you know that the strictest confidence will be observed, and through questions and challenges from the set members, your thinking should become clearer and a plan of action to overcome your difficulties will emerge. Having committed yourself to undertake the action and report back your findings to the set members at the next meeting, you have a clear time span in which to achieve the task. You know that excuses for non-action, and limp answers to probing questions as to why, will leave you exposed and vulnerable in the group. That thought alone should motivate you to achieve your goal!

We have outlined the ways of working of action learning sets in order to give you an idea of the principles under which they operate. They provide, in our view, a sound model for collaborative learning. We would encourage you, and other like-minded people, to consider the benefits of collaborative learning and to develop your own ways of working as a group or team. It may not be possible for you to operate in quite the same way as the action learning set, but it should still be possible to retain something of the ethical principles which that method enshrines.

EXERCISE
Consider whether there are any issues that are facing you at the moment which you are not sure how to resolve. Would the opportunity to share those issues with others in a supportive context be welcome? It might be worth asking one or two other people, perhaps from your church community or social circle, if they are in a similar position to yourself with issues to resolve but no one to share them with. If it proves to be the case, you might find that you have the beginnings of an action learning set on your hands!

ICT and collaborative learning

If you have a computer and are connected to the Internet, you may know that this has great potential for collaborative learning. Some university courses are now delivered exclusively through this method. Typically, online tutorials and seminars will be used, with learners contributing openly to the discussion. The writing of joint papers is also a feature of some courses, where individuals will contribute material which may then be critiqued and revised by others in an attempt to produce a more effective and refined piece of writing. There are also open discussions which you can access, probably by now on any topic you can think of! (If there is not a debate going on in the area that interests you, why not start one?) It is possible to ask questions of others who share your interests, and to contribute knowledge you have and ideas of your own, and to receive feedback on them from your partners in learning. (You might wish to refer back to chapter 2 for guidance on the use of the Internet for study purposes.)

Further reading

Bourner, T and Race, P (1990), *How to Win as a Part-Time Student*, London, Kogan Page (chapters 8 and 9).

McGill, I and Beaty, L (1992), *Action Learning: a practitioner's guide*, London, Kogan Page.

Northedge, A (1990), *The Good Study Guide*, Milton Keynes, Open University Press (chapter 3).

10. LEARNING FOR LIFE

Introduction

Most of us are familiar with the terms 'lifelong learning' and the 'learning society'. The publicity they have received may have brought to our attention the reality that, for all of us, learning is a lifelong process. We need to learn for life (emphasising, perhaps, the importance of schooling), but we also need to go on learning. While it is clear that to live is also to learn (though clearly 'amounts' of learning in relation to 'amounts' of living may vary considerably from individual to individual), we may be better advised to think of the idea of learning from living as a deliberate and purposefully chosen activity rather than as an ad hoc and incidental process, otherwise we may be in danger of demeaning the notion of learning. If all life is thought of as learning then we are likely to lose the meaning of what it is to learn.

Reflecting on experience

As you come near to the end of this book, consider what you have learnt so far through studying it. What skills have you developed? How will these skills be of use to you as you set out on your studies in theology, and in the broader areas of your life and work?

To what extent has your attitude to learning changed since you began studying this book? Do you now have a more positive view of yourself as a learner than before you started it?

Use the following set of questions as a way of assessing your progress to date: ▶▶

- Am I now more aware of what I know?
- Am I now more aware of what I can do?
- Do I value my skills and abilities and use them widely?
- Do I now consider alternative ways of doing things?
- Do I reflect on what I have done and consider how I could have done it better?

Lifelong learning

Lifelong learning, as a government initiative, means that learning opportunities should exist for *all* people whatever their social or employment status and whatever their age may be. In part it is about widening access to educational opportunities sufficiently to embrace all members of society. It is a recognition that people from certain socio-economic groups do not have a tradition of further and higher education, and it is about creating opportunities for them and helping and encouraging them to access learning for their own benefit and for the benefit of society at large. It is also a recognition that knowledge is changing so quickly and there has been such an explosion of knowledge that all of us need to be constantly in a state of learning if we are to remain employable and/or useful members of society. There is a partic-ular concern that advances in technology move at such a pace that as a nation, unless we take learning seriously, the economy will suffer and we will be in a state of social and economic decline. Gone are the days, we are told, when a job was for life. In this brave new world each of us will need to update our skills and knowledge on a constant basis if we are to be able to demonstrate our employability.

If you are about to embark upon a course of study, and it is the first time you have undertaken planned learning for a while, you are a good example of someone who is taking lifelong learning seriously. The concept of lifelong learning also means, however, that when you have completed this study programme you have not finished learning but have simply reached another stage in your lifelong learning agenda. Your next planned learning may not, however, be in higher education and so, in this chapter, we aim to focus on learning outside the academy and especially in such settings as everyday paid employment and voluntary work of various kinds, as well as learning in the church. We also recognise, of course, that your study programme is running concurrently with your life in general, and so we hope that much of what we have to say in this chapter will have immediate relevance for you. We reiterate the point that, for this to be considered 'learning from living' in a properly educational sense, at least some degree of intention to learn should be present or, better still, the learning should be planned for. This is in no way to deny that valuable learning may occur unexpectedly on many occasions, and we acknowledge that much learning, even in planned contexts of this sort, may occur spontaneously and unintentionally.

Changing face of higher education

Before we turn to learning beyond college or university, it may be worth considering briefly the changing face of higher education. This may help you to put your present study into context. The lifelong learning initiative is one example of a clear signal that the government wishes to have a greater say in shaping higher education for the future. There is no doubt that over the past two or three decades, successive governments have attempted to influence the way in which higher education is developing. We make this point, not because we wish either to applaud this influence or to denounce it, but to recognise it as a fact and to comment on some of its effects.

A dramatic increase in the participation rate in higher education over the past ten or so years means that higher education is no longer considered to be an élitist activity. In continuing to fund higher education from the public purse, governments have, in recent years, argued more strongly than ever before for a clear return on the public's investment. There is now an expectation that society in general, and the economy in particular, should benefit from higher education's output. This has, in turn, led to a change in understanding the nature of knowledge. If ever it was, it no longer seems acceptable to value knowledge only for its own sake (knowledge as an end in itself); there is also the expectation that those coming out of higher education will be able to *do* something with the knowledge they have acquired (knowledge as a means to an end). Whilst this has not yet led to a revolution in higher education, it is now commonplace for even the most arcane of disciplines to advertise ways in which a study of its mysteries will serve the student well in the world of work.

Of course, as far as some in higher education are concerned there may be little more than lip service paid to the idea. Even so, there is now a much greater awareness of the need to demonstrate that higher education serves a purpose beyond valuing knowledge for its own sake. Alongside the key areas of *research* (creating new knowledge) and *teaching* (passing on knowledge), a clear message is coming from higher education's paymasters that *application* (how to apply the knowledge gained) is to be a third major area of activity. To some degree, of course, there has always been an awareness of the role of higher education in preparing people for the world beyond the academy, and many programmes of study have always had a clear vocational orientation. Indeed the oldest and most venerated of academic institutions in this country were established in order to train people for the professions. The challenge now, however, is for *all* aspects of the university curriculum to demonstrate their applicability, and this will not, of course, happen overnight.

For a discipline such as theology, the issue of applicability may be seen as both straightforward and complex. It may be straightforward if thought of in terms of the narrower purpose of preparing individuals for various forms of vocational ministry, but complex if theology is to maintain its status as an independent non-vocational academic subject. Given the new terms of reference, the crucial question will be: *In what way does a study of theology enable an individual to make a real contribution to society and to the economy?*

Transferable skills

This leads us to consider an issue which has received considerable attention recently in higher education and that is the issue of so-called transferable skills. Sometimes in the higher education context these are referred to as higher order transferable skills. Essentially transferable skills are, as the name implies, skills which are developed in one context but can be applied in another. Increasingly employers, we are told, are seeking to employ graduates who are work-ready, and that means graduates who have been prepared by the university to *apply* the skills and competencies they have gained from their studies to the work situation. In cases where a graduate's degree studies do not relate directly to the employer's business activity, then clearly it is important to be able to demonstrate in what ways the degree is relevant to the workplace. Thus, if a typical employer wish-list includes employee skills in team-working, communication, self-reliance, critical thinking and so on, it is important that job applicants can provide evidence of ways in which their studies have enabled them to acquire these abilities.

We have included below a list of the transferable skills which we believe can be gained from a study of theology. It is not intended to be exhaustive but we hope it will give you some ideas about the ways in which the skills developed through a study of the discipline may have more general relevance and can be applied across (or 'transferred' to) a wide range of situations. The point we would make here is that, in addition to the knowledge of theology which you will gain from your study, you will also develop skills and competencies *through* a study of the discipline (for example, the ability to analyse, synthesise, evaluate and generally become a critical thinker). In some situations in which you may find yourself, the two will work comfortably together (for example, taking an active role in church life); in others, the skills gained from study can be drawn out of that context and *applied* elsewhere (for example, in your working life). Whereas knowledge may fade, the skills and competencies you develop will last and will be further enhanced as you use them in a variety of situations.

During the course of your studies you may wish to refer back to this list to identify and reflect on those skills and attitudes which we suggest you should be developing as a direct result of studying theology and which, we are claiming, are also transferable to other contexts. You could use it as a check-list in relation to the various modules or courses you take to see if indeed you are being given opportunities to develop in these areas.

We have organised the transferable skills and attitudes which are developed through a study of theology within seven main categories: written communication, oral communication, research, interpersonal, personal, reflective, and analytical/critical.

Written communication
- ability to *select* the appropriate means of conveying information, ideas and arguments
- essay-writing
- summarising
- reviewing books
- writing minutes/reports
- ability to précis documents or select what is significant

Oral communication
- ability to *listen*, to *think* about what is being said, and to *reply* to it effectively

- discussion
- giving explanations
- presenting information
- presenting arguments

Research
- ability to gather information from a variety of sources
- familiarity with information and communication technology
- awareness of sources of information and skills of retrieval

Interpersonal
- ability to work with and relate to others
- working as a member of a team
- 'contracts'
- appreciating the other's viewpoint
- readiness to stick by one's views
- resolve in the face of difficulties

Personal
- ability to work independently
- self-organisation
- setting goals
- meeting deadlines
- time management
- prioritising
- setting standards for oneself
- developing self-knowledge
- reliability
- enthusiasm
- commitment
- motivation
- persistence
- attention to detail
- self-reliance
- decision-making

Reflective
- ability to reflect at depth on issues of belief
- taking seriously the search for meaning in one's own and others' lives
- standing back from one's own 'faith' position/stance for living

- empathy
- insight

Analytical/critical
- ability to absorb new ideas and apply them
- evaluation of evidence
- evaluation of claims
- evaluation of attitudes
- synthesising skills
- problem-solving
- research topics
- interpretation
- contextualisation
- understanding the symbolic

EXERCISE

Having studied the above, pause at this point in your reading to:
- consider which of the skills and attitudes listed you already feel confident that you possess in some measure;
- identify the 'contexts' in which you use them (for example, work, church, home and family).

A self-audit of this kind can be rewarding because it makes you realise how skilled you already are. It should also help you to identify areas where you may not, at present, be particularly well skilled, as well as areas where further skill development is needed.

You may consider it worth while to record your self-audit in your Learning Journal (see chapter 7), then, as you progress with your studies, you can note down *when* and *in what context* you used a particular skill. This may help you to gauge the extent to which 'transferability' is occurring and give you an appreciation of the wider benefits of your study of theology.

Consider whether a study of theology offers anything unique by way of skill development or whether the same set of skills and attitudes could be acquired through the study of another humanities discipline (for example, History or English Literature). It may ▶▶

---

even be the case that making an assessment of the value of a study of theology in terms of transferable skill development is useful to you in future job applications or when seeking to take on more responsibility within your own church. You will be in a position where you can point to *evidence* of skill development. In any case, to know about your own learning development is, of course, also important in terms of your role as manager of your own learning.

The model of a reflective practitioner

We hope that, throughout this book, we have encouraged you to think about your learning achievements to date, to value them, and to build upon them. We hope that while you are studying, and when you have completed your course of study, you will recognise your own development and be able to take whatever 'academic' skills you have acquired into the world beyond the academy. In particular, your study should help you to increase your powers of *critical thinking* so that you will recognise unsubstantiated opinion and expose it for what it is, that you will question your own and other people's underlying assumptions, that you will consider a range of alternative solutions to a problem, demonstrating flexibility in your thinking, that you will keep an open mind where it is appropriate to do so, and so on. Such an approach to life and to living is valuable whether in the study, at work, in church life and social settings, or within the context of the home and the family. The skills associated with critical thinking should enable you to work more effectively on your own and with others, and help you to arrive at creative solutions to challenges that face you.

We hope that through studying this book, you will have become more aware of some of the strategies available to you to bring about and implement change and to further your learning. Whether at work or in the church, the model of *action learning* may be particularly appropriate to adopt, especially where there is collective responsibility for bringing about change. The method of action learning virtually mirrors that of the *experiential learning cycle*. From direct experience or awareness, a problem is identified. Through reflection on the problem a diagnosis is made (that is, the nature of the problem is determined). In considering how to resolve the matter a prognosis is arrived at (that is, a strategy is devised for overcoming the problem). Finally, action is taken (that is, the path to overcoming the problem is followed).

Perhaps the next time there is an issue to resolve at work or at church, you might suggest the model of action learning as a way of dealing with it. Combining forces with a number of other people who share your concern to deal with an issue may lead to fruitful dialogue, mutual encouragement to see the job through, and the acceptance of shared responsibility for the outcome, and ownership of it.

The model of the reflective practitioner is also a useful one to adopt in the context of work and/or church. The willingness to subject practice to critical thought implies a desire both to keep one's ways of working under review with an eye to improvement, and to keep an open mind on alternative strategies so that more radical solutions can be implemented if deemed appropriate. A considerable degree of flexibility and adaptability are key qualities of the reflective practitioner, whose concern is to get the job done as effectively and as efficiently as possible.

The responsibilities of being a critical thinker

In this final section of the book we would ask you to consider the extent of the responsibilities which 'membership' of the learning society places upon you. For whose benefit is the study programme which you are about to undertake? Is it for you alone or does it have wider implications? What responsibilities will becoming a more critical thinker place upon you?

In his book, *Developing Critical Thinkers*, Stephen Brookfield (1987) outlines a wide variety of contexts in which critical thinking can be applied. He argues that all of us have a responsibility to apply critical reasoning to all aspects of our lives. Critical thinking is necessary, in his view, to sustain a healthy democracy and to maintain a sound economy, thus making it a requirement of citizenship. In the preface to his book, Brookfield (1987, p. ix) has this to say:

> When we become critical thinkers we develop an awareness of the assumptions under which we, and others, think and act. We learn to pay attention to the context in which our actions and ideas are generated. We become skeptical of quick-fix solutions, of single answers to problems, and of claims to universal truth. We also become open to alternative ways of looking at, and behaving in, the world. The ability to think critically is important for our lives in many different ways.

When we are critical thinkers within our intimate relationships we learn to see our own actions through the eyes of others. At our workplaces we seek to exercise democratic control over workplace functions and organization and to take initiative in charting new directions and in designing the form and content of our activities. We become aware of the potential for distortion and bias in media depictions of our private and public worlds. Politically, we value freedom, we practise democracy, we encourage a tolerance of diversity, and we hold in check the demagogic tendencies of politicians.

What Brookfield does, in a sense, is to apply the skills of critical thinking to the world outside the academy which is, of course, the world that all of us inhabit. Because this is the world in which we all 'live and move and have our being', our perspective is not that of a detached academic observer but one of full involvement in the world. This means that our rational judgements are not divorced from our feelings and emotions. We therefore necessarily adopt a holistic approach to critical thinking, involving our intuitions as well as our logical and rational analyses. As Brookfield (1987, p. 14) observes, 'critical thinking is a lived activity, not an abstract academic pastime'. Reginald Revans (1982), whose developmental work on action learning has provided a platform for later thinkers, also argues that experiential learning of this sort involves the whole being, including the religious and spiritual dimensions of human being. This means that critical thinking in the world has a passionate edge to it; it is about being free and staying free; it is about liberation. Paulo Freire (1972) shares this same understanding of critical thinking. It provides the basis for his dialogical model of education developed against a background of oppressive government and extreme poverty. This is not so much about an approach to classroom-based schooling, though it could be applied in such contexts, but is principally about educating people to overcome the issues that are causing them disablement and the regimes that are keeping them oppressed. This is an education for liberation.

The dialogical model of education is essentially about the application of knowledge, that is, taking action in specific situations or contexts. It is an approach which requires the student to accept responsibility for his or her own learning, regarding teachers as facilitators and partners in learning. It requires a reflective approach whereby actions are subjected to critical appraisal. Because learning is not divorced from life, the student needs to engage fully with the learning process in a holistic way, bringing all aspects of life to bear on an issue. This is a dynamic model of education which is not restricted to the completion of a syllabus but has to be engaged in throughout a lifetime of learning.

EXERCISE

As a final exercise, pause for a moment to reflect on what all of this might mean for you. Perhaps you had not anticipated that 'doing a bit of study' in theology would have such implications and lay upon you such responsibilities! Taking those responsibilities seriously will necessarily increase your involvement in a whole range of activities which have potential for learning whether at work, at home or in the church.

Spend a few moments now jotting down some examples that you are aware of from your own experience of work, home or church where it would be desirable for this dynamic model of education to operate.

Here are some prompts to get you started.
- What is your experience of church as 'community'?
- Is there opportunity for learning and for growth in this direction?
- What learning does your work organisation need to undergo in relation to the application of its own stated policies and mission?
- To what extent, for example, is it deemed to be sufficient to have a written statement of policy without monitoring its implementation?

You will, no doubt, find plenty of examples from your own experience to reflect on and examine for their potential as learning opportunities both for yourself and for others.

Conclusion

We hope that we have encouraged you in your studies and provided you with some of the tools that you will need in order to achieve success. We hope that from your studies you will carry with you something of the spirit of the dialogical model of education. While we value knowledge for its own sake (knowledge as an end in itself), we do not believe that the *application* of knowledge (knowledge as a means to an end) demeans its status. In fact, in our view, application enhances the status of knowledge. It means that knowledge has the potential to bring about *transformations*. Knowing 'that' and knowing 'how' are opposite sides of the same coin; one is not the poorer relation of the other. We hope that you will use the knowledge and the skills that you will gain from your academic study to bring about positive transformations in your own lives and in the lives of others.

Further reading

Brookfield, S D (1987), *Developing Critical Thinkers*, Milton Keynes, Open University Press.

Freire, P (1972), *Pedagogy of the Oppressed*, Harmondsworth, Penguin.

Schön, D A (1987), *Educating the Reflective Practitioner*, San Francisco, California, Jossey-Bass.

REFERENCES

Atkinson, D J and Field, D H (eds) (1995), *Dictionary of Christian Ethics and Pastoral Theology*, Leicester, IVP.

Barton, J (ed.) (1998), *The Cambridge Companion to Biblical Interpretation*, Cambridge, Cambridge University Press.

Brookfield, S D (1987), *Developing Critical Thinkers*, Milton Keynes, Open University Press.

Brown, R E, Fitzmyer, J A and Murphy, R E (eds) (1991), *The New Jerome Biblical Commentary*, London, Geoffrey Chapman.

Childress, J (ed.) (1986), *A New Dictionary of Christian Ethics*, London, SCM.

Clarke, P (ed.) (1996), *A Dictionary of Ethics, Theology and Society*, London, Routledge.

Coggins, R J and Houlden, J L (eds) (1990), *A Dictionary of Biblical Interpretation*, London, SCM.

Cross, F L and Livingstone, E A (eds) (1997), *The Oxford Dictionary of the Christian Church*, Oxford, Oxford University Press.

Davies, J G (ed.) (1986), *A New Dictionary of Liturgy and Worship*, London, SCM.

Douglas, J D (1965), *New Bible Dictionary*, Leicester, IVP.

Douglas, J D (ed.) (1978), *The New International Dictionary of the Christian Church*, Grand Rapids, Michigan, Zondervan.

Dunn, J G D (1995), *1 Corinthians*, Sheffield, Sheffield Academic Press.

Eliade, M (ed.) (1987), *The Encyclopedia of Religion*, London, Macmillan.

Evans, R (1999), *Using the Bible: studying the text*, London, Darton, Longman and Todd.

Freire, P (1972), *Pedagogy of the Oppressed*, Harmondsworth, Penguin.

General Synod Liturgical Commission (1989), *Making Women Visible: the use of inclusive language with the ASB*, London, Church House Publishing.

Green, J B, McKnight, S and Marshall, I H (1992), *Dictionary of Jesus and the Gospels*, Leicester, IVP.

Gordon, R P (1998), *1 and 2 Samuel*, Sheffield, Sheffield Academic Press.

Hastings, J, Selbie, J A and Gray, L H (eds) (1908), *Encyclopaedia of Religion and Ethics*, Edinburgh, T and T Clark.

Hawthorne, G F, Martin, R P and Reid, D G (1993), *Dictionary of Paul and His Letters*, Leicester, IVP.

Herrmann, N (1993), *The Creative Brain*, Lake Lure, North Carolina, Brain Books.

Hodgson, P C and King, R H (eds) (1985), *Readings in Christian Theology*, London, SPCK.

Hodgson, P C and King, R H (1994), *Christian Theology: an introduction to its traditions and tasks* (revised edition), Philadelphia, Pennsylvania, Fortress Press.

Honey, P and Mumford, A (1986), *The Manual of Learning Styles* (fifth edition), Maidenhead, Peter Honey.

Isherwood, L and McEwan, D (eds) (1996), *An A to Z of Feminist Theology*, Sheffield, Sheffield Academic Press.

Johns, E and Major, D (1991), *Witness in a Gentile World: a study of Luke's Gospel*, Cambridge, Lutterworth Press.

Kolb, D A, Rubin, I M and Osland, J S (1991), *Organised Behaviour: an experiential approach* (fifth edition), London, Prentice Hall.

Komonchak, J (ed.) (1987), *The New Dictionary of Theology*, London, Gill and Macmillan.

McGrath, A (ed.) (1993), *The Blackwell Encyclopedia of Modern Christian Thought*, Oxford, Blackwell.

McGrath, A (1994), *Christian Theology: an introduction*, Oxford, Blackwell.

McGrath, A (1995), *The Christian Theology Reader*, Oxford, Blackwell.

Mays, J L (ed.) (1988), *Harper's Bible Commentary*, New York, Harper.

Metzger, B (ed.) (1993), *The Oxford Companion to the Bible*, Oxford, Oxford University Press.

Myers, A C (ed.) (1987), *The Eerdman's Bible Dictionary*, Grand Rapids, Michigan, Eerdmans.

Revans, R W (1982), *The Origins and Growth of Action Learning*, Lund, Sweden, Chartwell-Bratt.

Richardson, A and Bowden, J (eds) (1983), *A New Dictionary of Christian Theology*, London, SCM.

Rogers, C (1983), *Freedom to Learn*, New York, Charles E Merrill.

Woodward, J (ed.) (1998), *The Blackwell Reader in Pastoral Theology*, Oxford, Blackwell.

Applying for the Church Colleges'
Certificate Programme

The certificate programme is available in Anglican Church Colleges of Higher Education throughout England and Wales. There are currently hundreds of students on this programme, many with no previous experience of study of this kind. There are no entry requirements. Some people choose to take Certificate courses for their own interest and personal growth, others take these courses as part of their training for ministry in the church. Some go on to complete the optional assignments and, after the successful completion of three courses, gain the Certificate. Courses available through the *Exploring Faith: theology for life* series are ideal for establishing ability and potential for studying theology and biblical studies at degree level, and they provide credit onto degree programmes.

For further details of the Church Colleges' Certificate programme, related to this series, please contact the person responsible for Adult Education in your local diocese or one of the colleges at the addresses provided:

The Administrator of Part-time Programmes, Department of Theology and Religious Studies, Chester College, Parkgate Road, CHESTER, CH1 4BJ ☎ 01244 375444

The Registry, Roehampton Institute, Froebel College, Roehampton Lane, LONDON, SW15 5PJ ☎ 0181 392 3087

The Registry, Canterbury Christ Church University College, North Holmes Road, CANTERBURY, CT1 1QU ☎ 01227 767700

The Registry, College of St Mark and St John, Derriford Road, PLYMOUTH, PL6 8BH ☎ 01752 636892

The Registry, Trinity College, CARMARTHEN, Carmarthenshire, SA31 3EP ☎ 01267 676804 (direct)

Church Colleges' Programme, The Registry, King Alfred's College, Sparkford Road, WINCHESTER, SO22 4NR ☎ 01962 841515

Part-time Programmes, The Registry, College of St Martin, Bowerham Road, LANCASTER, LA1 3JD ☎ 01524 384529